OCS Report
MMS 2000-022

Deepwater Gulf of Mexico:
America's Emerging Frontier

I0448301

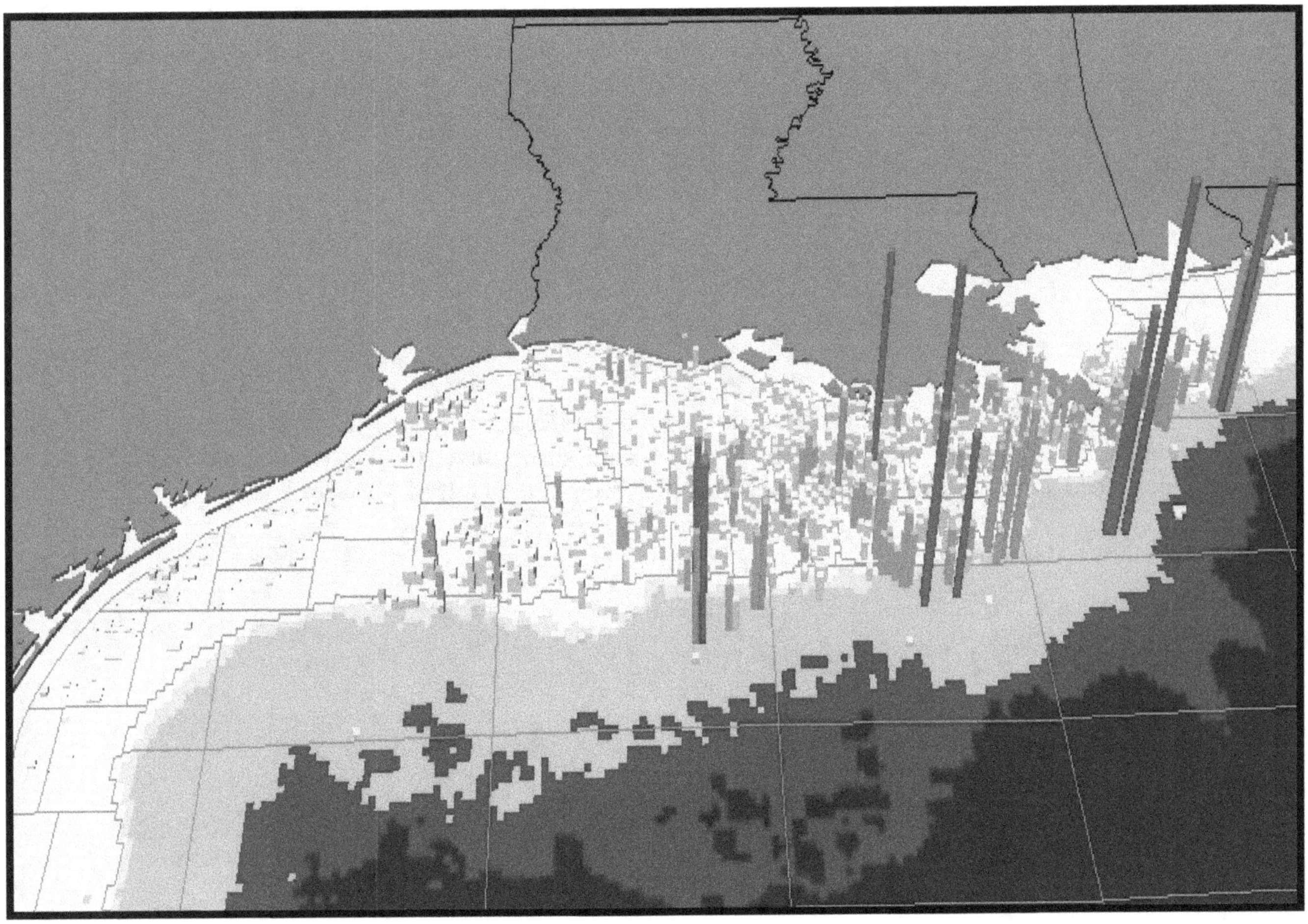

MMS **U.S. Department of the Interior**
Minerals Management Service
Gulf of Mexico OCS Region

ON COVER—Maximum historical oil production rates for Gulf of Mexico wells. Taller bars indicate higher production rates. The data show numerous deepwater oil wells produced at significantly higher rates than ever seen in the Gulf of Mexico.

OCS Report
MMS 2000-022

Deepwater Gulf of Mexico: America's Emerging Frontier

Richie D. Baud
Robert H. Peterson
Carey Doyle
G. Ed Richardson

U.S. Department of the Interior
Minerals Management Service
Gulf of Mexico OCS Regional Office

New Orleans
April 2000

Contents

Figures

Table | **Page**

vii

Preface

The deepwater of the Gulf of Mexico has emerged as a world class oil and gas province in the last four years. Leasing, exploration, and production activity accelerated rapidly since MMS first published MMS Report 97-0004 in 1997 to herald the arrival of the deepwater of the Gulf of Mexico as America's new frontier.

In 1999, total Gulf of Mexico oil production reached an estimated 494 million barrels after hovering around 300 million barrels a year for much of the decade. The increase has come from the deepwater and was highlighted in late 1999, when oil production from the deepwater portion of the Gulf of Mexico exceeded that of the shallow water for the first time in history. This historic change after 53 years of production in the Gulf of Mexico has been driven by several major factors all coalescing in the late 1990's.

High flow rate wells have driven the economics of projects and acted as a strong incentive to explore and develop deepwater leases. The use of subsea well completions has also contributed to the economics of deepwater projects. At the end of 1999 there were 186 subsea completions—62 of them in deepwater—and they accounted for 25 percent of all deepwater oil production and 40 percent of deepwater gas production.

The deepwater Gulf has also seen a number of major technical and engineering achievements. These achievements include such projects as subsea production in 5,000+ feet of water (Mensa, 1997), TLP production in 3,800 feet of water (Ursa, 1999), the first spar production (Neptune, 1997), and the first mini-TLP production (Morpeth, 1998).

These technological advances, when combined with incentives passed by Congress under the Deepwater Royalty Relief Act of 1995, have also led to a tremendous surge in deepwater leasing. This act provided automatic royalty relief to new oil and gas leases issued during 1996-2000. Between 1996 and 1999 more than 3,000 new leases were issued in water depths of 200 meters or greater in the Gulf of Mexico, with more than 2,600 of these in 800 meters of water or greater.

With 30 fields on production at the end of 1999, the deepwater of the Gulf of Mexico can rightly claim to be America's new frontier and has truly emerged as a world class hydrocarbon province. Its future looks bright, as many new geologic trends are only now seeing the first exploratory drilling. Truly, the deepwater will drive the new millenium.

Chris C. Oynes
Regional Director
Minerals Management Service

Introduction

The deepwater Gulf of Mexico (GOM) has recently emerged as an important oil and gas province and an integral part of the Nation's oil and gas supply. A major milestone occurred in late 1999 when more oil was produced from the deepwater GOM than from the shallow-water GOM. This trend in increasing deepwater (water depths greater than or equal to 1,000 ft) production is expected to continue, along with high levels of exploratory drilling, development activity, pipeline construction, and shore support activities. Deepwater GOM field discovery sizes have been several times larger than the average shallow-water field discoveries. The deepwater fields have also been some of the most highly prolific producers in the GOM.

This report is divided into five sections.

The **Introductory** section discusses
- highlights of current deepwater GOM activity.

The **Leasing** section discusses
- historical water depth and bidding trends in deepwater leasing,
- lease holdings of major oil companies compared with nonmajor oil companies,
- the impact of company mergers on deepwater exploration, and
- future deepwater lease activity.

The **Drilling and Development** section discusses
- deepwater rig activity,
- historical drilling statistics,
- the transition to deeper wells and deeper water,
- deepwater development systems including subsea completions, and
- the progress of deepwater infrastructure development.

The **Reserves and Production** section discusses
- historical deepwater reserve additions,
- historical trends in deepwater production,
- deepwater production from various companies, and
- high deepwater production rates.

The **Summary and Conclusions** section discusses
- increasing deepwater oil and gas production and anticipated new fields,
- large future reserve additions associated with recently announced discoveries,
- discoveries in new, lightly tested plays with large potential,
- expected future increases in deepwater discoveries based on drilling of the large deepwater lease inventory,
- limited deepwater rig availability,
- long lag times between leasing, drilling, and initial production, and
- difficulties evaluating deepwater leases before their terms expire.

The Gulf of Mexico OCS is divided into the Western, Central, and Eastern Planning Areas (figure 1). The analysis in this report focuses on the Central and Western areas. Many of the data presented in this report are subdivided according to water depth. These divisions (1,000, 1,500, 5,000, and 7,500 ft) are illustrated in figure 1, along with the congressionally mandated Deepwater Royalty Relief (DWRR) zones (200, 400, and 800 m) for reference. For purposes of this report, we define deep water as greater than or equal to 1,000 ft-water depth.

A few other definitions are useful at this point:

- *Proved Reserves* are those quantities of hydrocarbons that can be estimated with reasonable certainty to be commercially recoverable from known reservoirs. These reserves have been drilled and evaluated and are generally in a producing or soon-to-be producing field.
- *Unproved Reserves* can be estimated with some certainty (drilled and evaluated) to be potentially recoverable, but there is as yet no commitment to develop the field.
- *Known Resources* in this paper refer to discovered resources (hydrocarbons whose location and quantity are known or estimated from specific geologic evidence) that have less geologic certainty and a lower probability of production than the Unproved Reserves category.
- *Industry-Announced Discoveries* refer to oil and gas accumulations that were announced by a company or otherwise listed in industry publications. These discoveries have not been evaluated by MMS and the reliability of estimates can vary widely.

More detailed definitions may be found in the annual *Estimated Proved and Unproved Oil and Gas Reserves, Gulf of Mexico, December 31, 1997* report (Crawford et. al., 2000).

Throughout this report we refer to several deepwater fields by their nicknames. Appendix A provides locations, operators, and additional information regarding these fields. Note that the field's identifying block number corresponds to the first lease qualified by MMS as capable of production. Note also that the term "oil" refers to both oil and condensate throughout this report and "gas" includes both associated and nonassociated gas.

When the original version of this report (Cranswick and Regg, 1997) was published in February 1997, a new era for the GOM had just begun with intense interest in the oil and gas potential of the deepwater areas. There were favorable economics, recent deepwater discoveries, and intense leasing at that time. In February 1997 there were 16 producing deepwater fields, up from only 5 at the end of 1992. Industry was rapidly advancing into deepwater and many of the anticipated fields have begun production since the 1997 report.

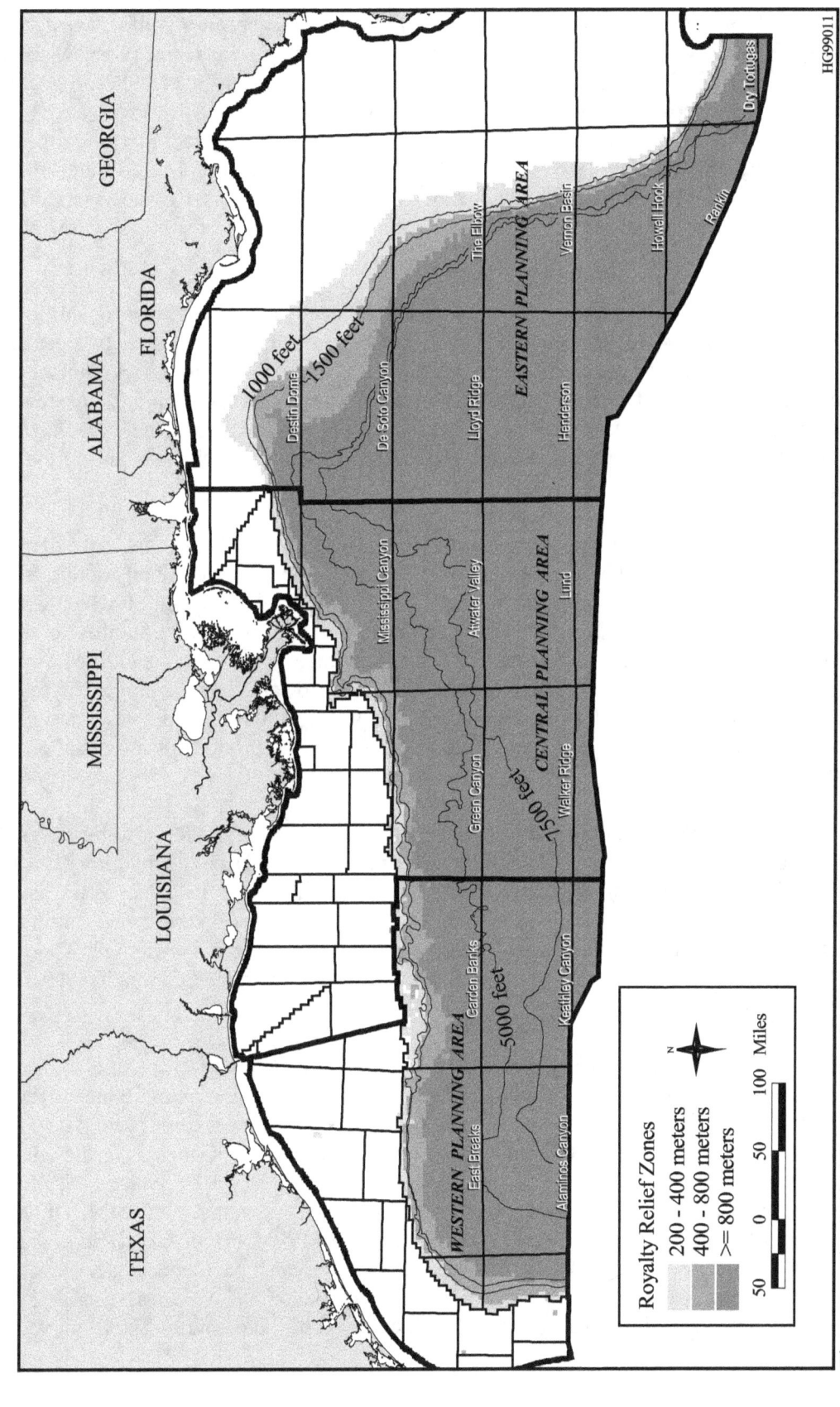

Figure 1. - The Gulf of Mexico OCS is divided into Western, Central, and Eastern Planning Areas. Water depth categories used in this report are shown in addition to shaded Deep Water Royalty Relief zones.

3

At the end of 1999, there were 30 producing fields in the deepwater Gulf of Mexico, up 30 percent in just 12 months and up 88 percent since the original report (Cranswick and Regg, 1997). In 1998 deepwater oil production rose 47 percent over 1997 production, and in 1999 deepwater oil production increased an additional 41 percent over 1998 production. Similarly, deepwater gas production increased 47 percent in 1998, followed by a 51 percent jump in 1999. Although U.S. oil production declined about 410,000 barrels a day from 1994 to 1998, the decline would have been nearly twice as large if the deepwater GOM production had not increased by 321,000 barrels a day (Minerals Management Service, 1999).

The dramatic shift toward high activity levels in the deepwater GOM occurred during the last few years. This recent shift, however, has been developing for over two decades. Deepwater production began in 1979 with Shell's Cognac field, but it took another five years before the next deepwater field (Exxon's Lena field) came online. Deepwater exploration and production continued to grow at an ever-increasing rate, leading to a flurry of activity in the past five years. This report focuses on changes during the last eight years, 1992-1999.

The growth in deepwater activity spans all phases of exploration and development, including leasing, drilling, and production. There are approximately 7,600 active leases in the Gulf of Mexico Outer Continental Shelf (OCS), 48 percent of which are in deepwater. (Note that lease statuses may change daily, so the current number of active leases is an approximation.) Contrast this to approximately 5,600 active Gulf of Mexico leases in 1992, only 27 percent of which were in deepwater. On average, there were 27 rigs drilling in deepwater in 1999, up from only 3 rigs in 1992. Likewise, deepwater oil production rose about 550 percent and deepwater gas production increased almost 800 percent from December 1992 to December 1999.

All phases of exploration and development moved steadily into deeper waters over the past eight years. We observed this trend in seismic activity, leasing, exploratory drilling, field discoveries, and production. Major oil companies dominated deepwater leasing activity until 1996, when nonmajors joined the trend. Major oil companies continue to dominate deepwater oil and gas production, but we expect production from nonmajors to surge in a few years, when anticipated discoveries on their 1996 through 1999 lease acquisitions begin production.

The OCS Deep Water Royalty Relief (DWRR) Act (43 U.S.C. §1337) had a significant impact on deepwater GOM activities. This legislation provides economic incentives for operators to develop fields in water depths greater than 200 meters (656 ft). These incentives include the automatic suspension of Federal royalty payments (for new leases issued in 1996-2000) on the initial 17.5 million barrels of oil equivalent (MMBOE) produced from a field in 200-400 meters (656-1,312 ft) of water, 52.5 MMBOE for a field in 400-800 meters (1,312-2,624 ft) of water, and 87.5 MMBOE for a field in greater than 800 meters (2,624 ft) of water. Reduction of royalty payments is also available through an application process for some deepwater fields that were leased prior to the DWRR Act but had not yet gone on production. The automatic suspension volume provision of the DWRR Act expires on November 28, 2000. Even if these incentives are altered or eliminated on future leasing, leases acquired between November 28, 1995, and November 28, 2000, will retain the incentives until their expiration.

The DWRR Act spurred a variety of deepwater activities. One of the first impacts was a dramatic increase in the acquisition of 3-D seismic data (figure 2). (Note that figures 2 and 3 illustrate areas permitted for seismic acquisition. The actual coverage available may be slightly different than that permitted.) Three-dimensional seismic data are huge volumes of digital energy recordings resulting from the transmission and reflection of sound waves through the earth. These large "data cubes" can be interpreted to reveal likely oil and gas accumulations. The dense volume of recent, high-quality data greatly reduces the inherent risks of hydrocarbon exploration. Figure 2 illustrates the recent surge of seismic activity in the deepwater Gulf of Mexico during the last eight years. Seismic acquisition has stepped into progressively deeper waters since 1992. Figure 3 shows the abundance of 3-D data now available. These data blanket most of the deepwater GOM, even beyond the Sigsbee Escarpment (a geologic and bathymetric feature in extremely deep water). Note that many active deepwater leases were purchased before these 3-D surveys were completed (only the more sparsely populated 2-D data sets were available).

Modern seismic data often generate new ideas leading to surges in leasing and drilling activity. Figure 4 illustrates several new deepwater plays in the GOM. Although the traditional deepwater mini-basin plays are far from mature (especially considering the recently announced Crazy Horse discovery in Mississippi Canyon Block 778), the Mississippi Fan Foldbelt, Perdido Foldbelt, and Tertiary Fan/Mesozoic Plays show that the deepwater arena is still very much a frontier area. Although sparsely tested, the Mississippi Fan Foldbelt Play shows great potential with announced discoveries at three locations (prospects Mad Dog in Green Canyon Block 826, Neptune in Atwater Block 575, and Atlantis in Green Canyon Block 699). The Perdido Foldbelt Play is essentially untested with only one shallow well in Alaminos Canyon Block 600 (Baha field). The Tertiary Fan/Mesozoic Play is heavily leased, but also remains untested. These new plays are large in areal extent, have multiple opportunities, and contain potentially huge structural and/or stratigraphic traps with the possibility of billions of barrels of hydrocarbons.

The DWRR Act also encouraged extensive leasing in the deepwater GOM. Figure 5 shows the recent history of deepwater leasing. Activity slowly increased from 1992 through 1995. Immediately after the DWRR Act was enacted, however, deepwater leasing activity exploded. (Other factors also contributed to this activity, including improved 3-D seismic data coverage, several key deepwater discoveries, the recognition of high deepwater production rates, and the evolvement of deepwater development technology.) Deepwater leasing activity slowed somewhat in 1998 and 1999, possibly because of low oil prices. Note also the gradual but continuous progression of leasing into deeper waters with time. The GOM leasing status is shown in figure 6. Shallow-water leasing is especially dense. The deepwater is also heavily leased, but some voids remain. There are about 3,930 active leases in water depths less than 1,000 ft, about

Figure 2. - Progressive deepwater 3-D seismic permit coverage from 1992 through 1999.

1994-1995

1998-1999

1992-1993

1996-1997

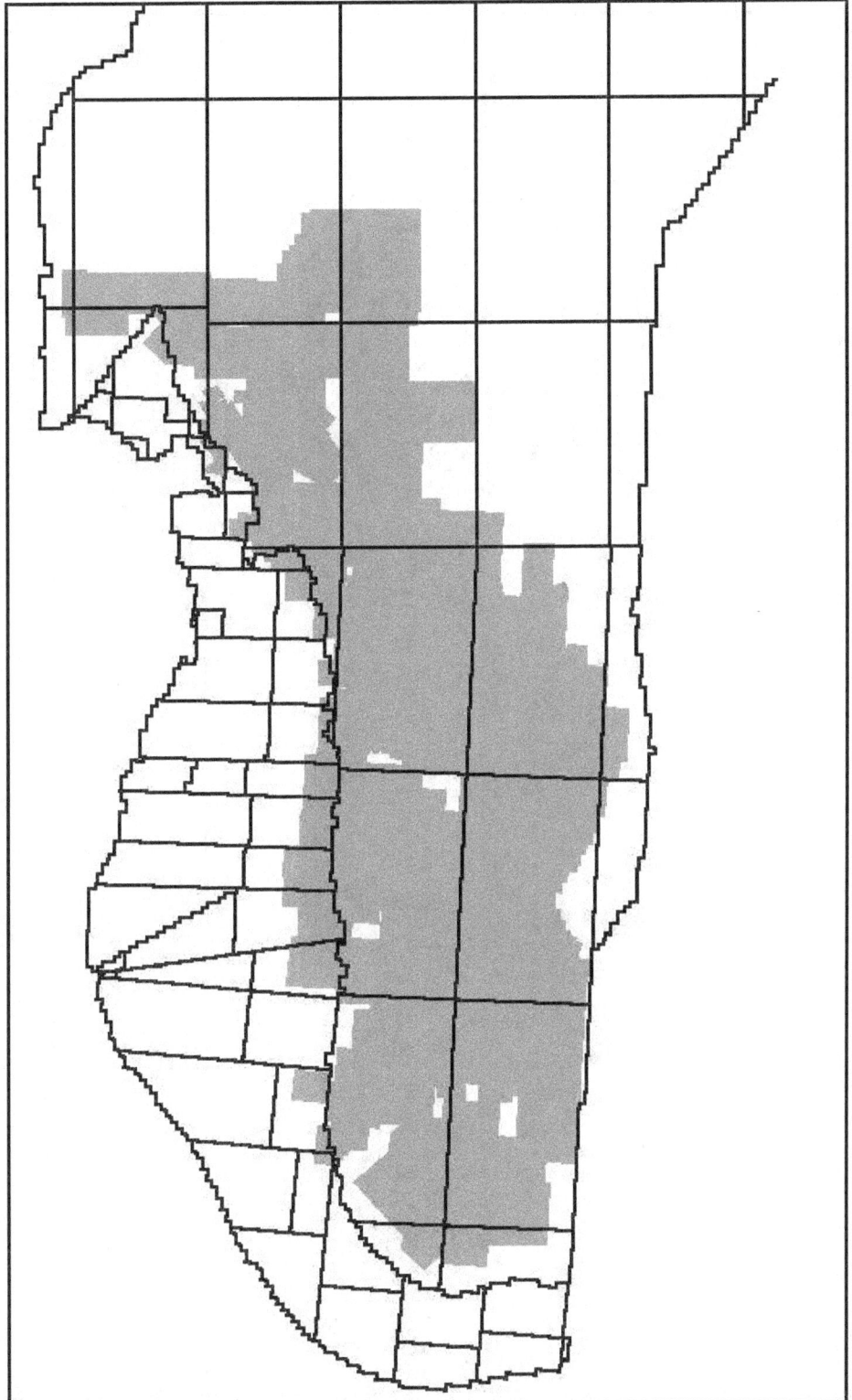

Figure 3. - Deepwater Gulf of Mexico 3-D seismic permit coverage from 1992 through 1999.

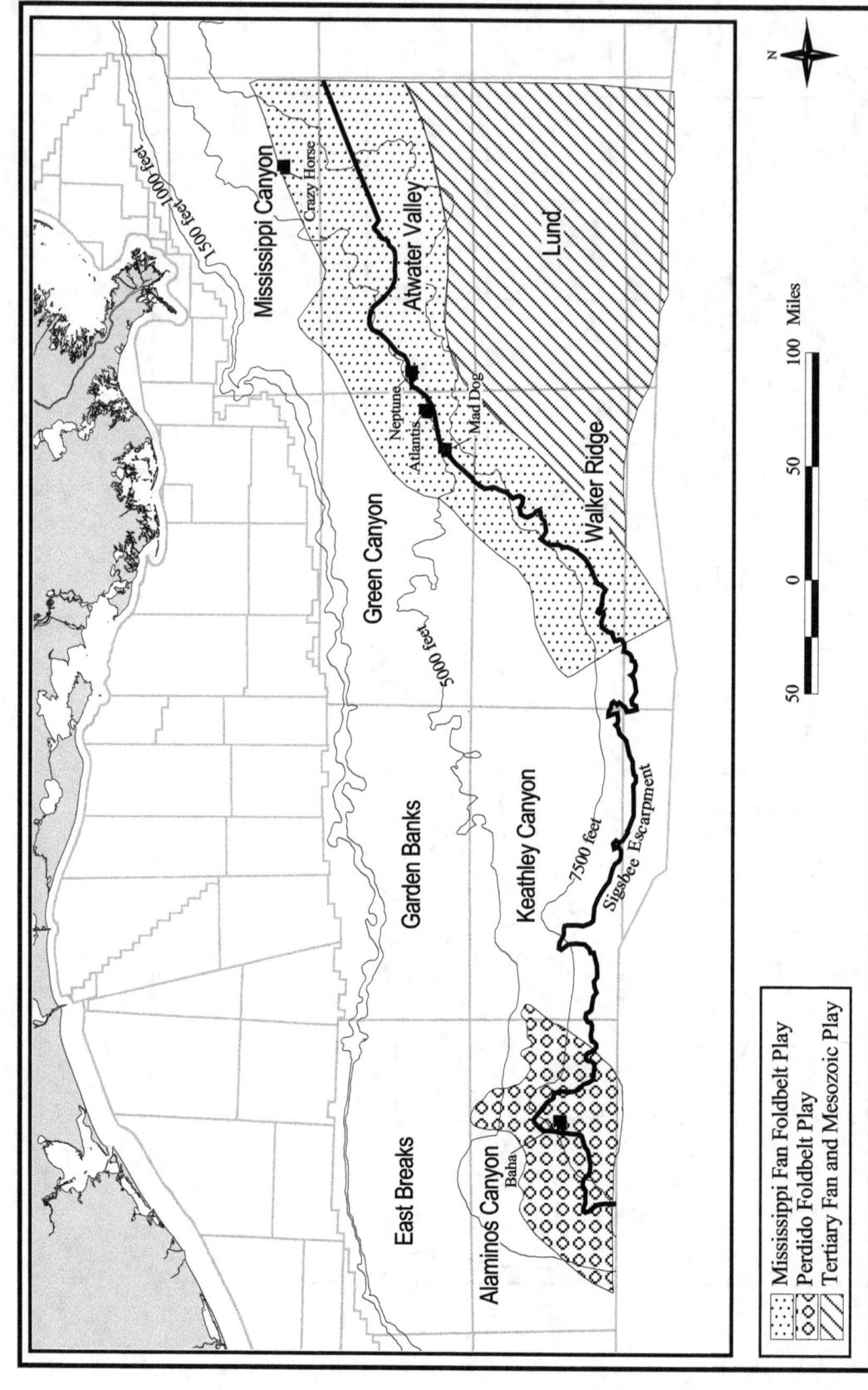

Figure 4. - New deepwater plays in the Gulf of Mexico.

8

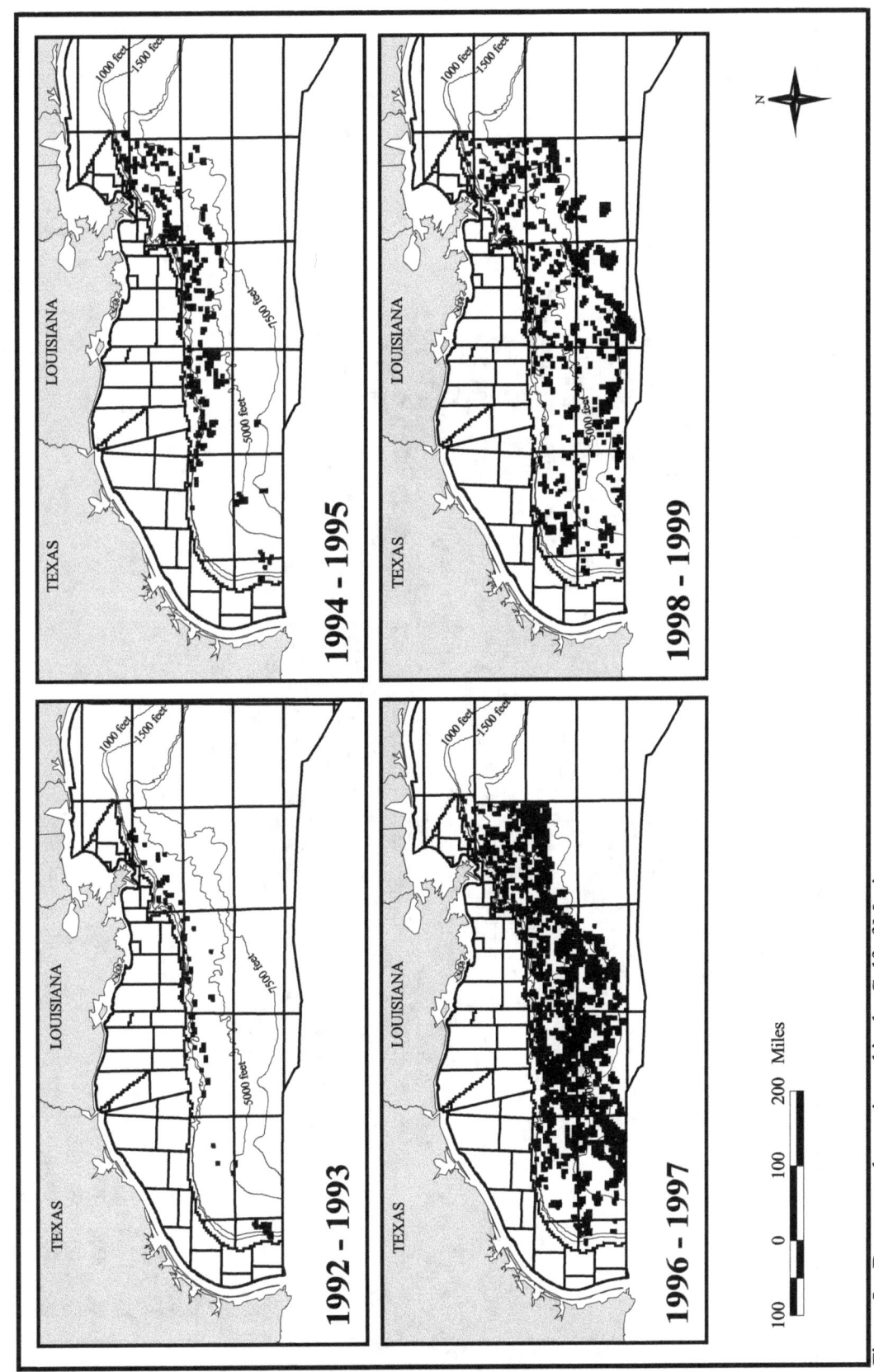

Figure 5. - Deepwater leases issued in the Gulf of Mexico.

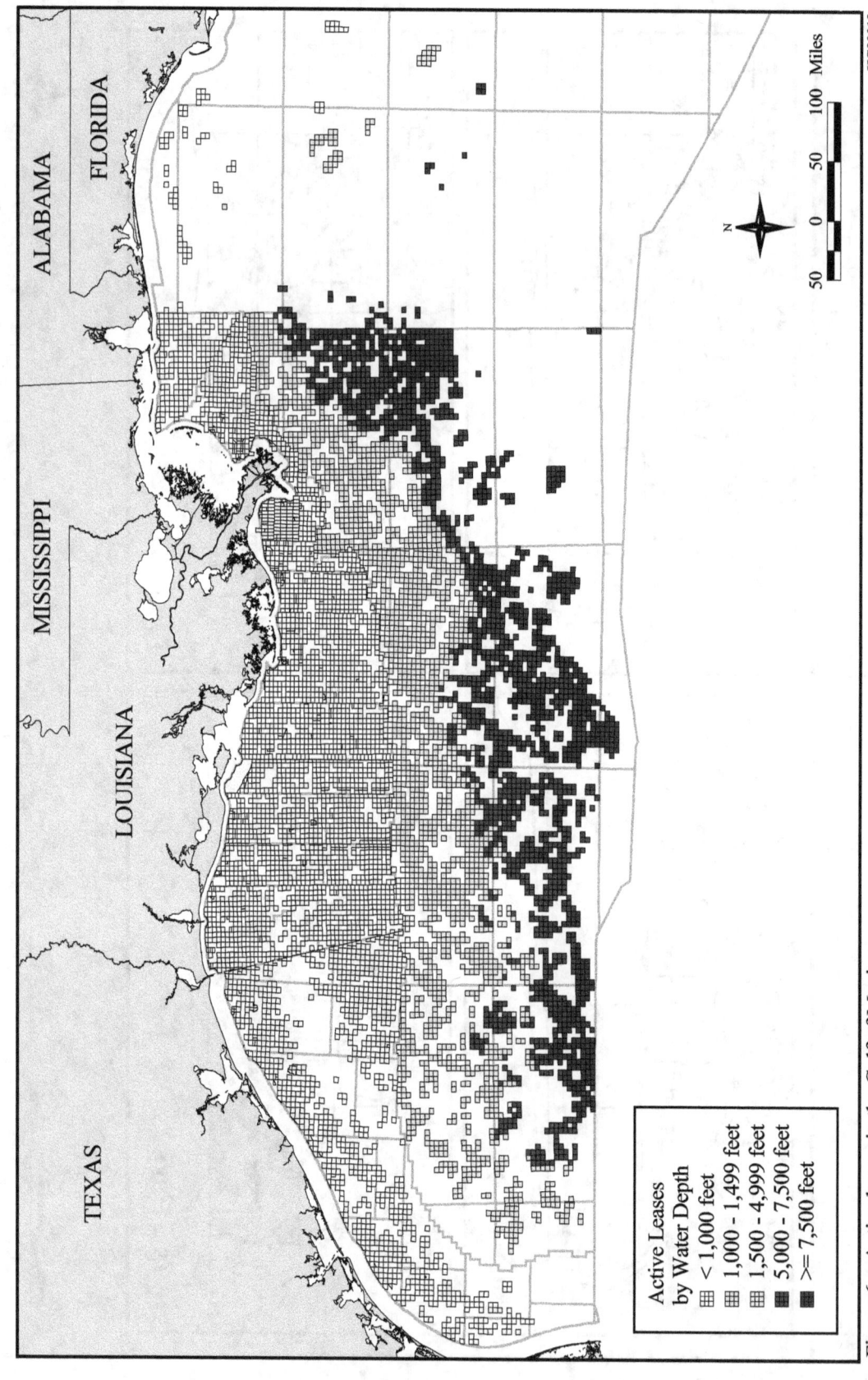

Figure 6. - Active leases in the Gulf of Mexico.

10

180 active leases in 1,000-1,499 ft water depth, about 1,830 active leases in 1,500-4,999 ft water depth, about 1,190 active leases in 5,000-7,499 ft water depth, and about 470 active leases in water depths of 7,500 ft and greater. The abrupt termination of active leases south of the Alabama-Florida state line is where the Eastern Planning Area begins. A lease sale in a portion of this planning area is scheduled to occur in 2001, the first Eastern Gulf lease sale since 1988.

Operators contend with numerous obstacles when venturing into the deepwater arena. Figure 7 illustrates many natural features and manmade zones that require special considerations for oil and gas activities. The Minerals Management Service (MMS) is currently conducting an environmental assessment (EA) on deepwater oil and gas activities; it will ensure that these activities occur in a technically safe and environmentally sound manner. Furthermore, the EA will identify and evaluate potential impacts from deepwater operations and develop potential measures to mitigate impacts from deepwater activities on the marine, coastal, and human environments.

In addition to environmental considerations specific to deepwater, significant financial obstacles exist. Deepwater operations are very expensive and often require significant amounts of time between the initial exploration and first production. A further constraint is the availability of drilling rigs capable of drilling deepwater wells (the number of ultra-deepwater rigs is especially limited).

Despite these obstacles, deepwater operators often reap great rewards. Figure 8 shows the history of discoveries in the Gulf of Mexico. There is a clear shift toward deeper water with time, and the number of deepwater discoveries continues at a steady pace. Note that the first frame of this figure represents a 10-year span, whereas the other frames represent 5-year spans. Figure 9 shows how major and nonmajor oil and gas companies compare in terms of deepwater discoveries. (Appendix B lists those companies defined as majors.) Leases that were majority-owned by major companies (when the discoveries occurred) are shown as black circles and leases majority-owned by nonmajor companies are shown as open circles. To date, majors account for about two-thirds of the deepwater discoveries. Additionally, discoveries by nonmajor companies tend to be in the shallower portions of the deepwater, while majors tend to dominate the ultra-deep frontier areas (at least to date).

In addition to the significant number of deepwater discoveries, the flow rates of deepwater wells and field sizes of deepwater discoveries are often quite large. These factors are critical to the economic success of deepwater development. Figure 10 illustrates the estimated sizes and distributions of 39 proved deepwater fields. In addition to their large sizes, deepwater fields have a wide geographic distribution and also range in geologic age from Pleistocene through Miocene and older.

The growing number of large deepwater fields on production requires increasing support from onshore service bases. Producing deepwater fields have service bases in southeast Louisiana (figure 11). Pending Plans of Exploration (POE's) and Development Operations Coordination Documents (DOCD's) filed with MMS indicate that support

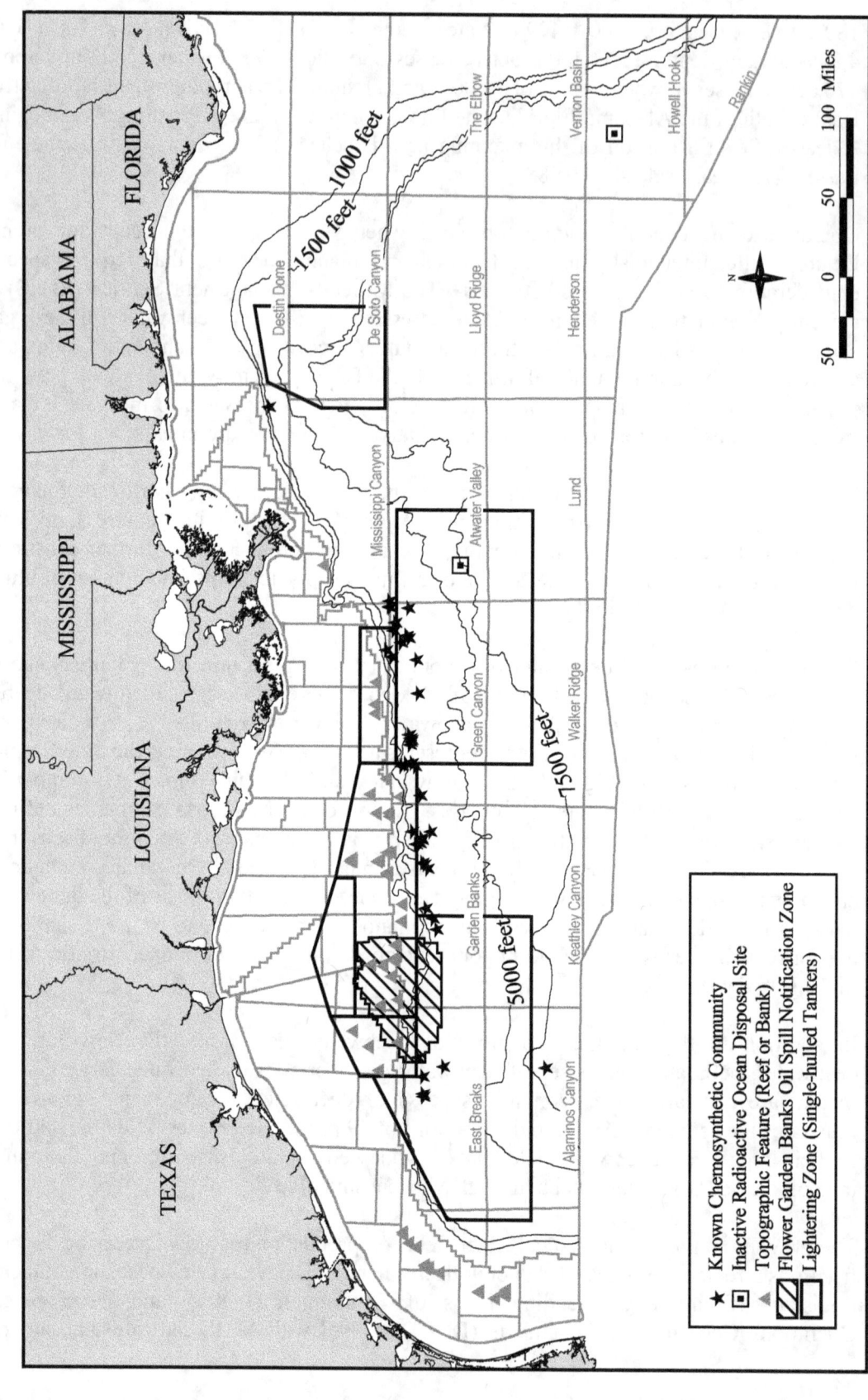

Figure 7. - Deepwater environmental and administrative features.

12

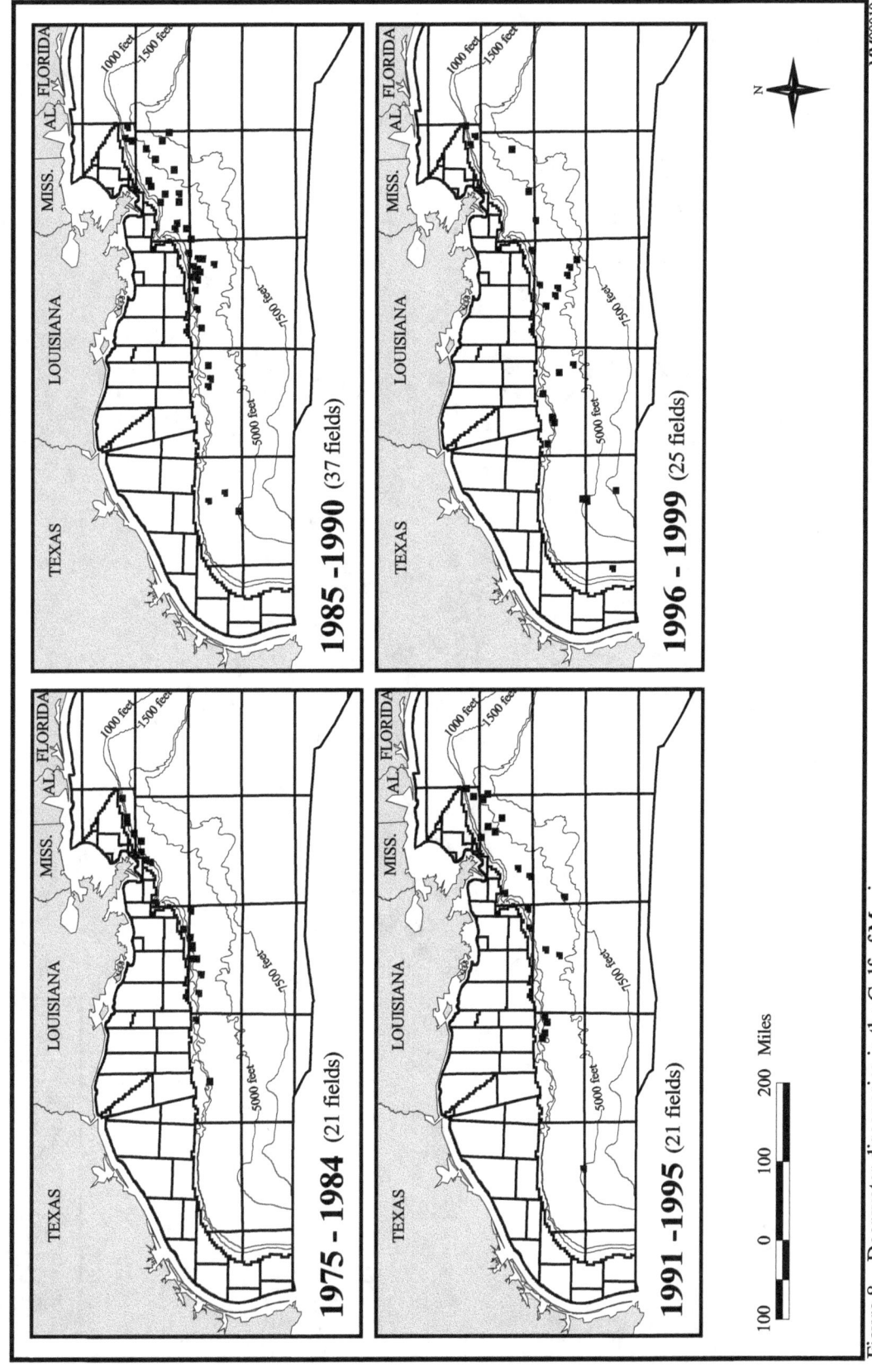

Figure 8. - Deepwater discoveries in the Gulf of Mexico.

MMS99019

13

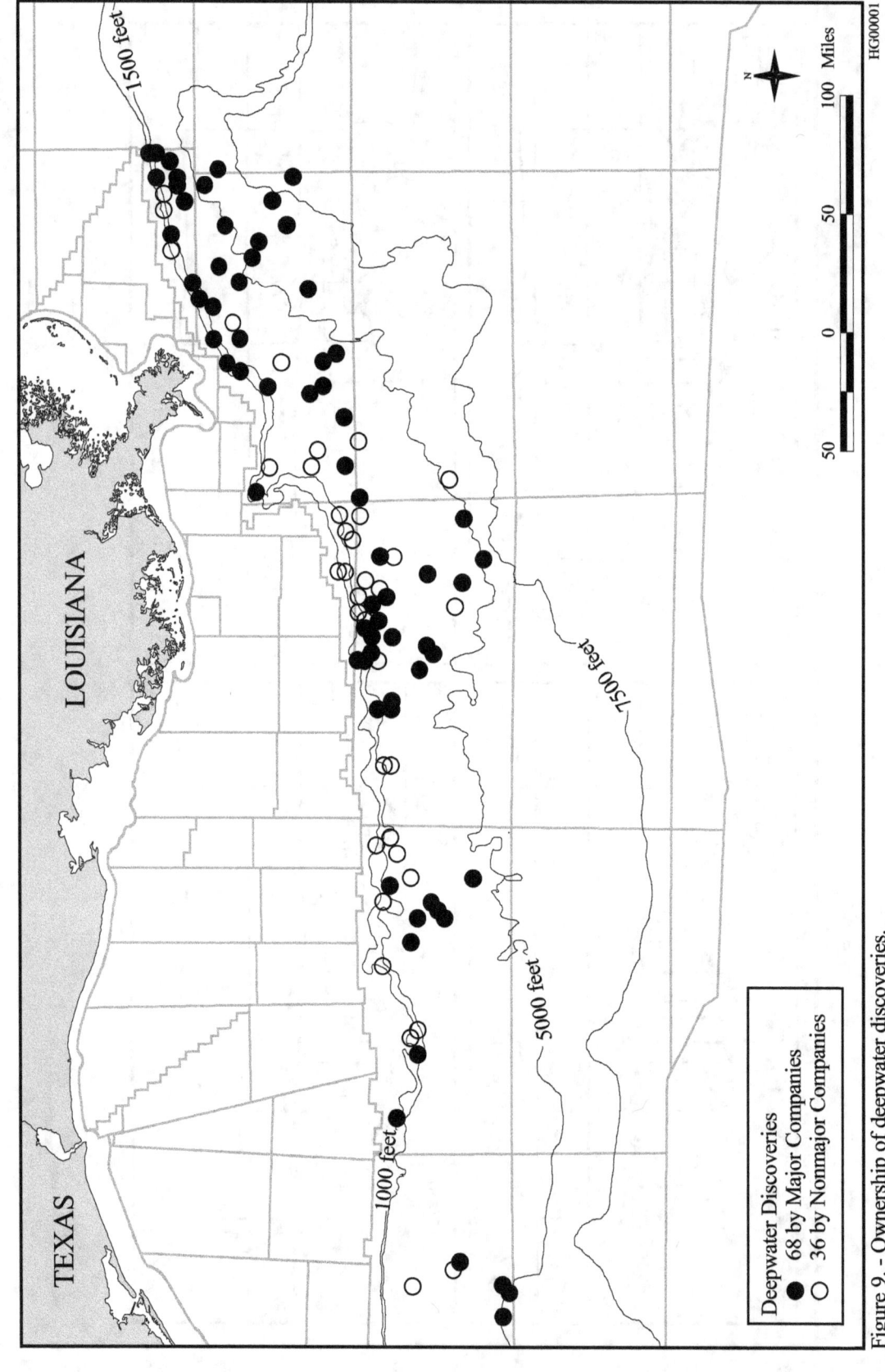

Figure 9. – Ownership of deepwater discoveries.

14

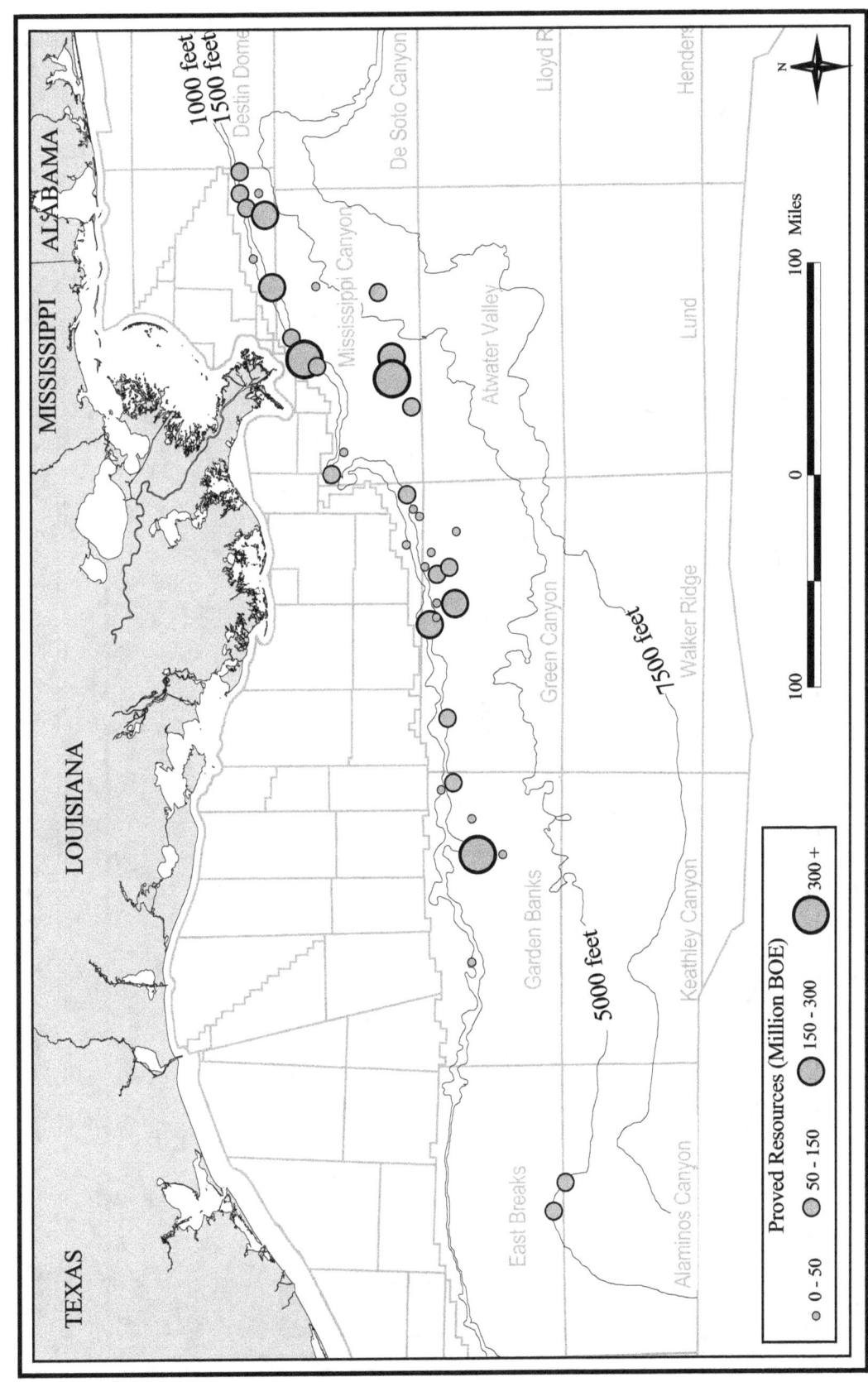

Figure 10. - Estimated volumes of 39 proved deepwater fields.

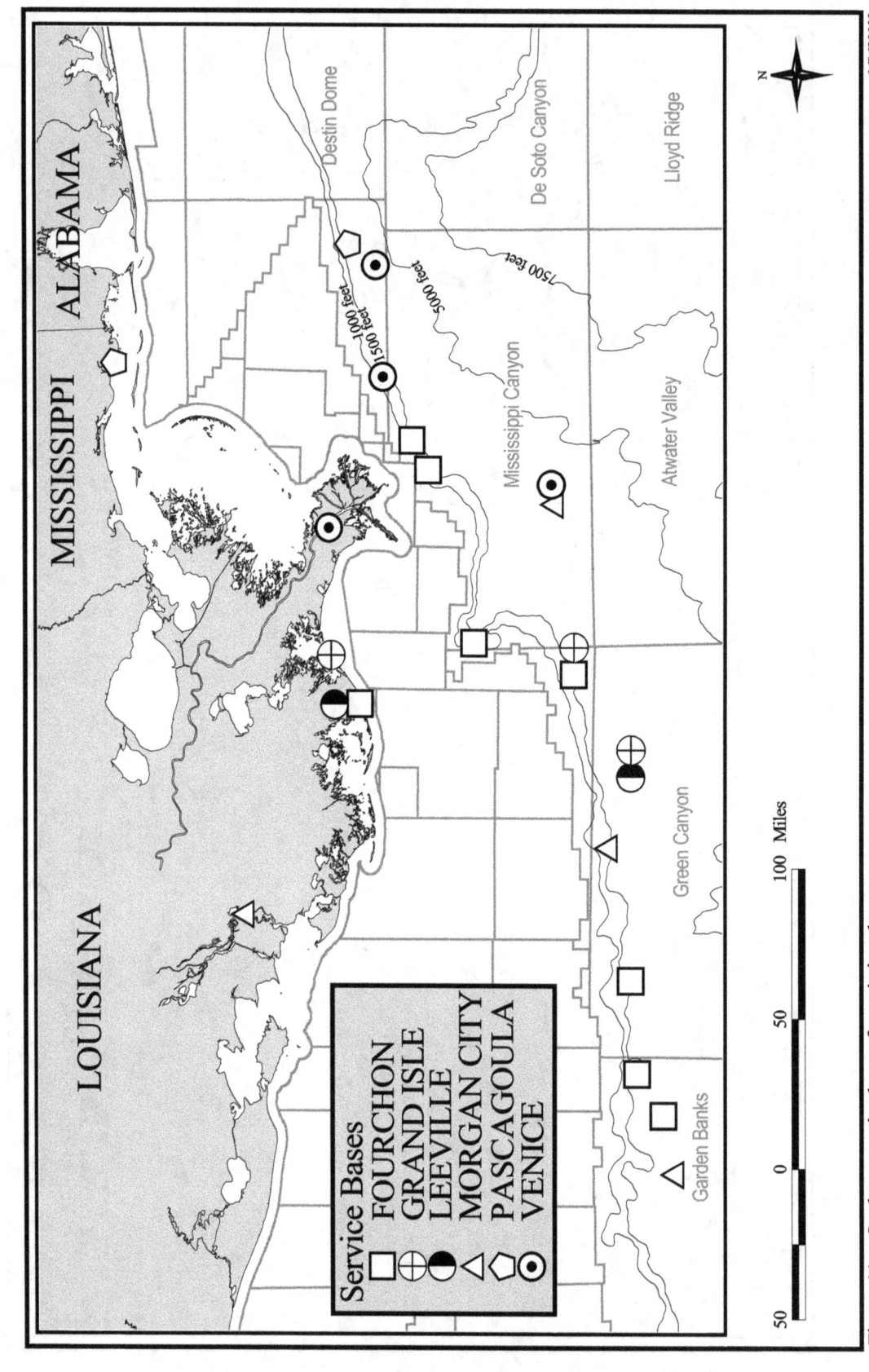

Figure 11. - Onshore service bases for existing deepwater structures.

16

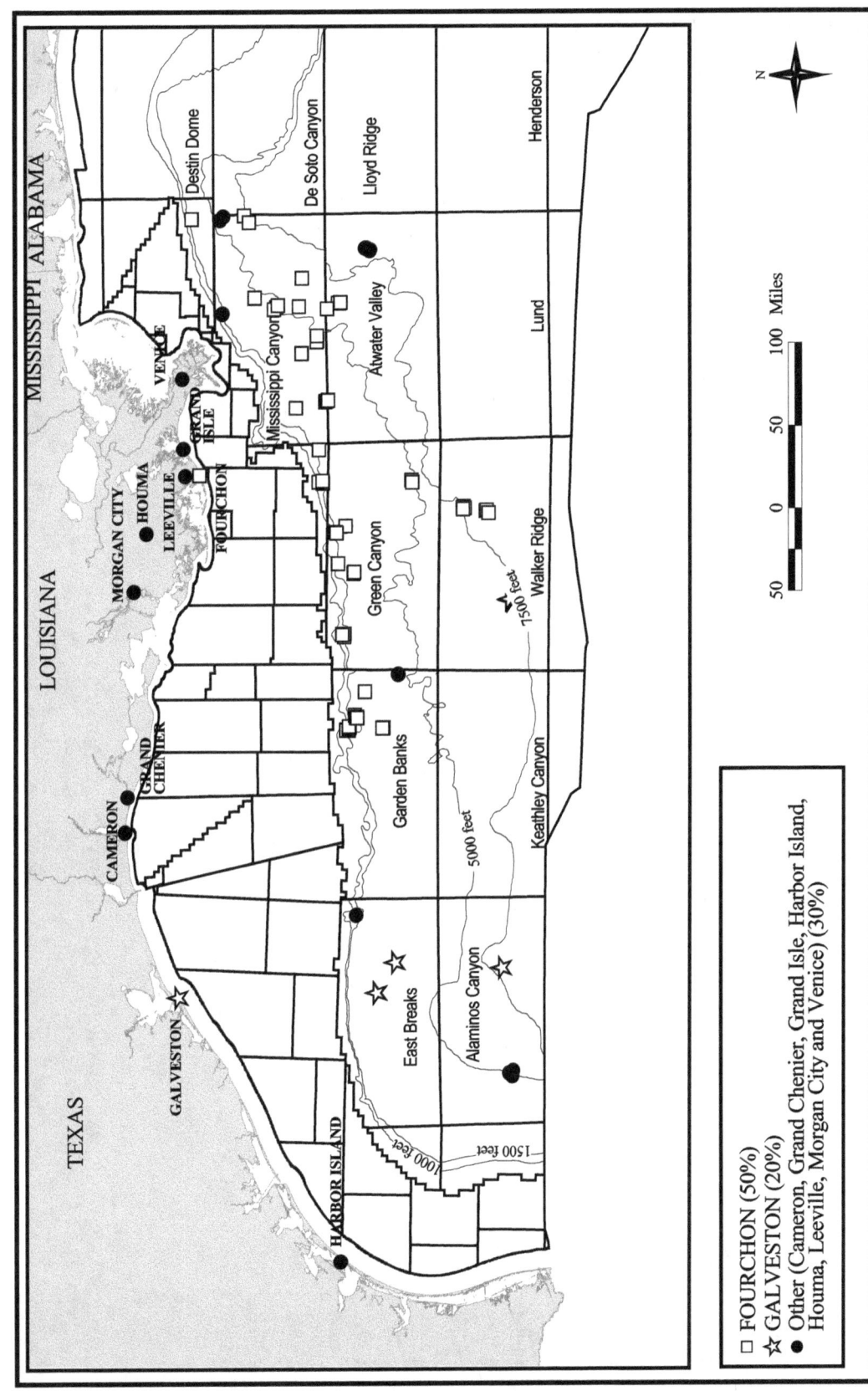

Figure 12. – Onshore service bases for pending deepwater plans.

from southeast Louisiana will grow significantly, and new support will come from southwest Louisiana and the Texas coast (figure 12). Although expanding along the Gulf Coast, shore-based support for deepwater operations is likely to remain concentrated in southeastern Louisiana.

The infrastructure needed to bring deepwater production online continues to develop over time. Figure 13 shows the framework of major oil and gas pipelines in the shallow-water GOM. Figure 14 illustrates the network of deepwater pipelines currently in place. The deepwater pipeline infrastructure grew rapidly over the past few years to keep pace with the expanding number of deepwater fields.

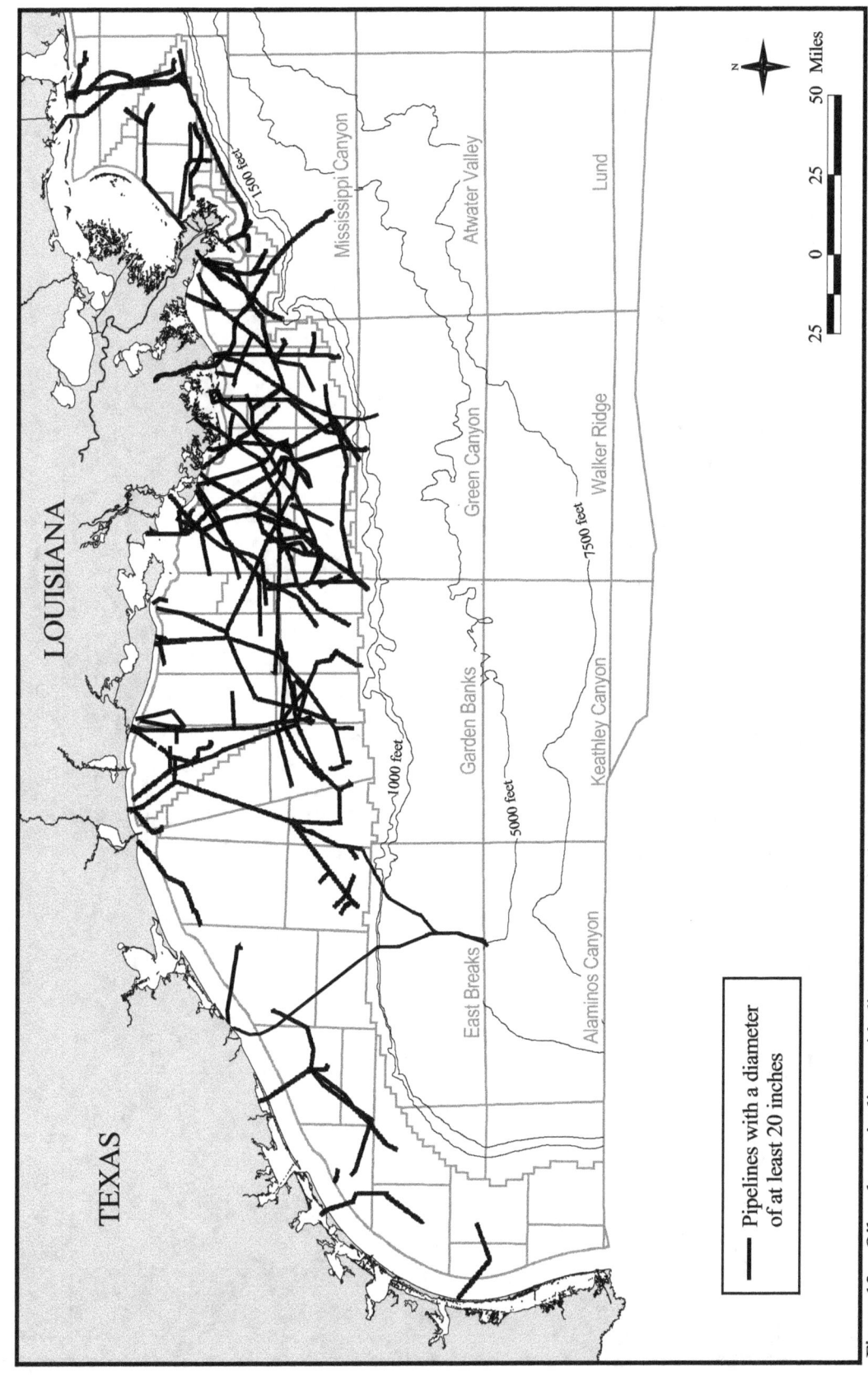

Figure 13. - Oil and gas pipelines with diameters greater than or equal to 20 inches.

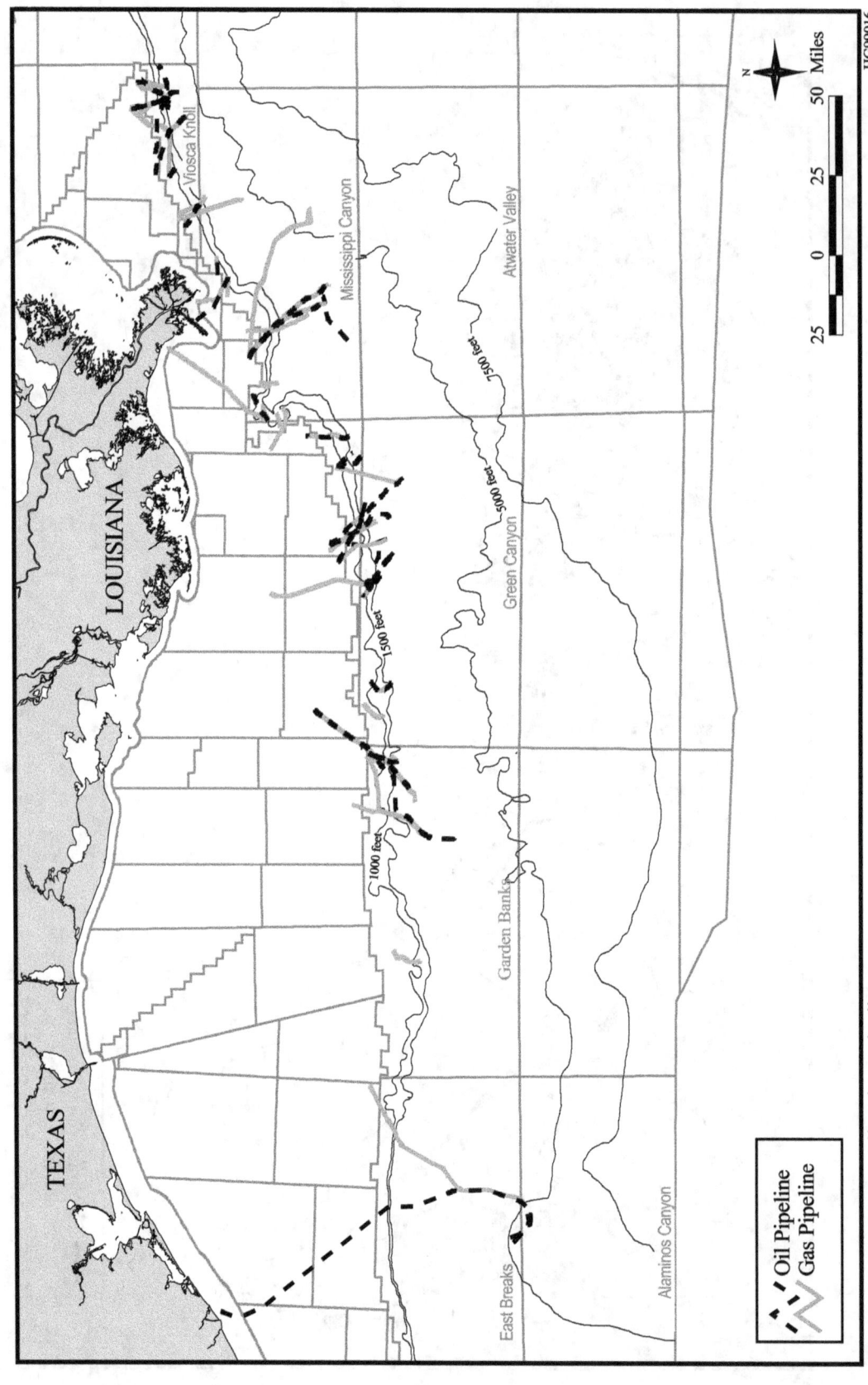

Figure 14. – Deepwater oil and gas pipelines.

Leasing

Leasing activity in the deepwater GOM increased steadily in the early 1990's and exploded in 1996 because of, in part, the economic incentives introduced in the Deep Water Royalty Relief (DWRR) Act. Figure 15 shows the magnitude of the DWRR impact, with tremendous deepwater leasing activity from 1996 to 1998 in water depths greater than 800 meters (where the greatest royalty relief is available). The boom in deepwater leasing was also enhanced by the evolvement of deepwater technology, several large deepwater discoveries, and excellent production rates coming from deepwater fields.

The water depth categories depicted in figure 15 are based on the divisions used in DWRR. This figure includes shallow- and deepwater leasing trends for an 8-year period. Figure 16a was derived from the data in figure 15, but displays the deepwater categories used elsewhere in this report (shallow-water data are excluded from figure 16a). These deepwater data show the rapid increase in leasing activity that began in 1995 (primarily in the 1,500-4,999 ft water depths) and exploded in 1996 (throughout the deepwater). Figure 16b shows the total amount of money bid in each water depth range since 1992. Large financial investments were made from 1996 through 1998, with sharp spending increases in water depths greater than 5,000 ft. Figure 16c combines the data in figures 16a and 16b to reveal the average bid price of deepwater leases through time. The average bid price for all deepwater leases steadily increased from 1994 through 1998, particularly in water depths greater than 1,500 ft. In fact, the average bid price for ultra-deepwater tracts (greater than or equal to 7,500 ft water depth) rose to levels comparable with leases in less than 5,000 ft water. This is likely due to several discoveries in water depths approaching 7,500 ft, very large structural traps in these areas, and the improved feasibility of developing ultra-deepwater fields. Note that figures 16a-c reflect all blocks that received bids (including those that were rejected).

As the value of deepwater leases increased throughout the 1990's, the MMS rejected an increasing number of deepwater high bids that it viewed as insufficient (figure 17). Apparent also in figure 17 is the fact that tracts with rejected bids moved into increasingly deeper waters in the late 1990's. From 1992 through 1995, almost all rejected bids were on the shelf. In 1996-1997, bid rejects were evenly divided between shallow- and deepwater. In 1998-1999, however, the majority of bid rejects were in deepwater. This trend reflects the fact that, as more deepwater fields began production, they provided analogs (with high production rates, thick reservoir sections, and production infrastructure), and thus reduced the risk on deepwater sale blocks, leading to the increased net present worth of many unleased blocks.

A handful of major oil and gas companies blazed the trail into deepwater in the 1980's and early 1990's. In this report, we define major companies to include Arco, BP Amoco, Chevron, Exxon Mobil, Shell, and Texaco. Appendix B breaks this list down further, showing the companies and subsidiaries we combined to form these six majors. (Our grouping of these six does not indicate a regulatory conclusion or an analysis of

21

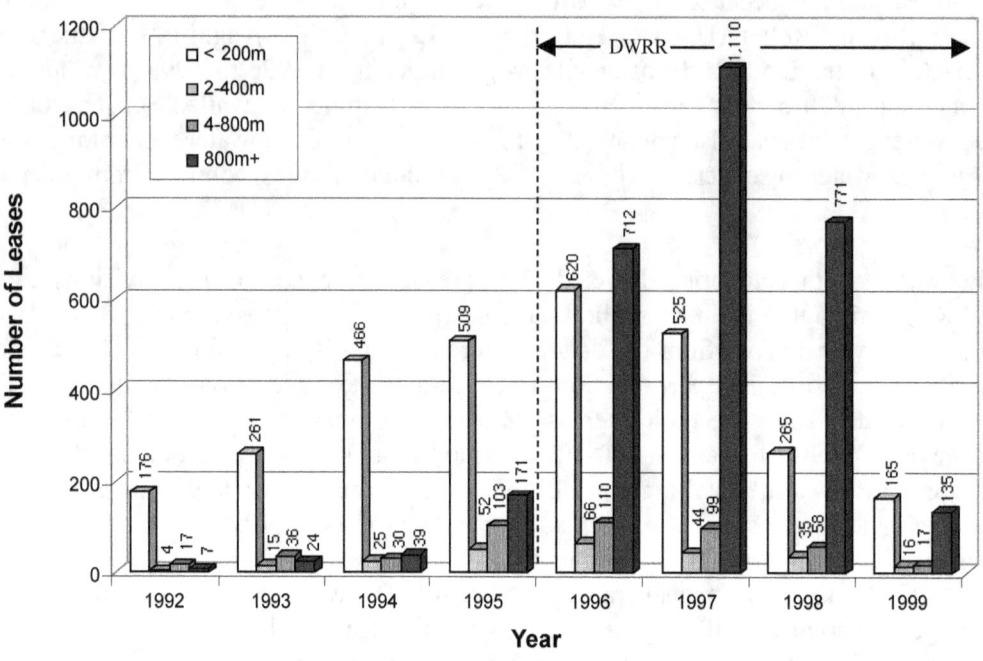

Figure 15. - Number of leases issued each year subdivided by DWRR water depth categories.

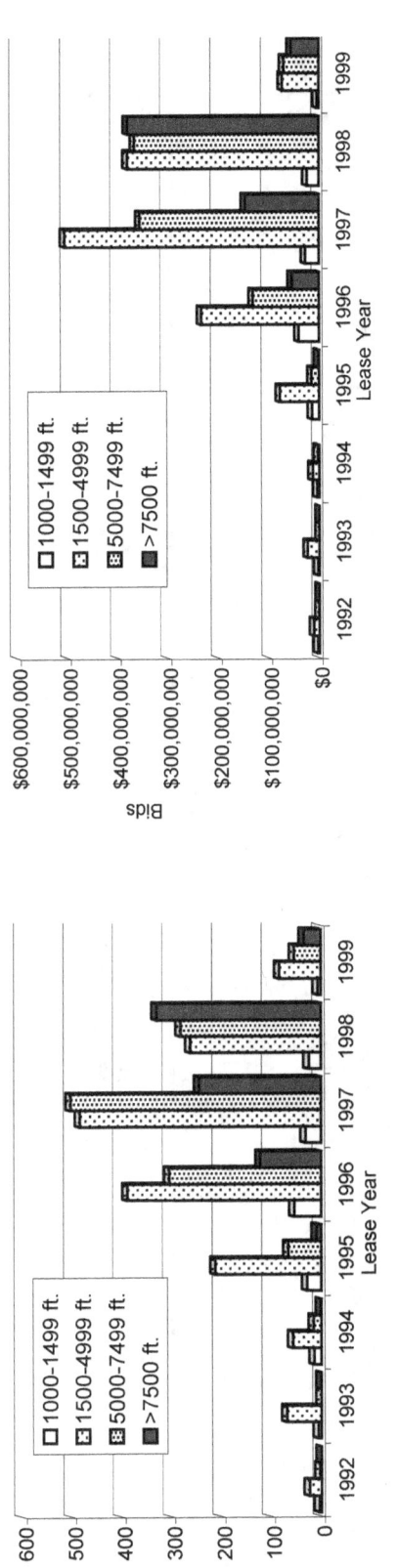

Figure 16b. - Total bid amounts in deepwater intervals.

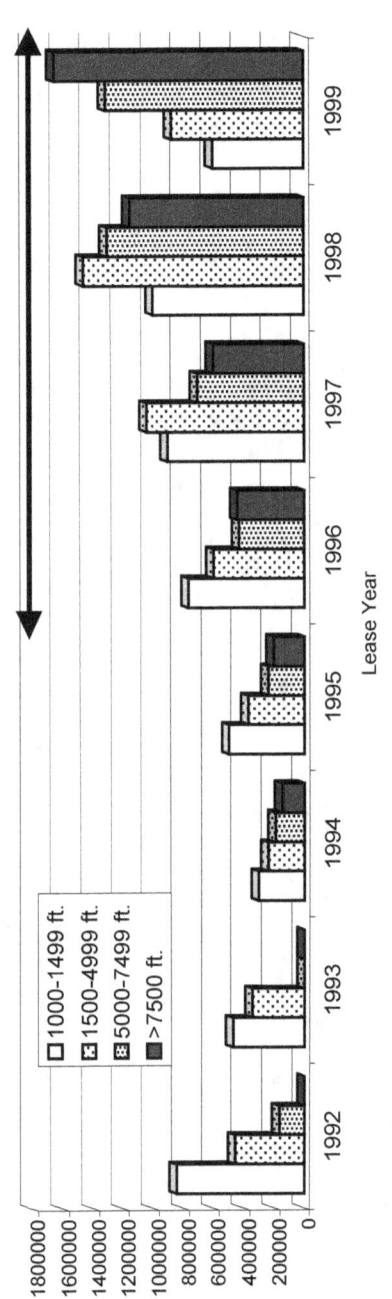

Figure 16c. - Average bid amount per block in deepwater intervals.

23

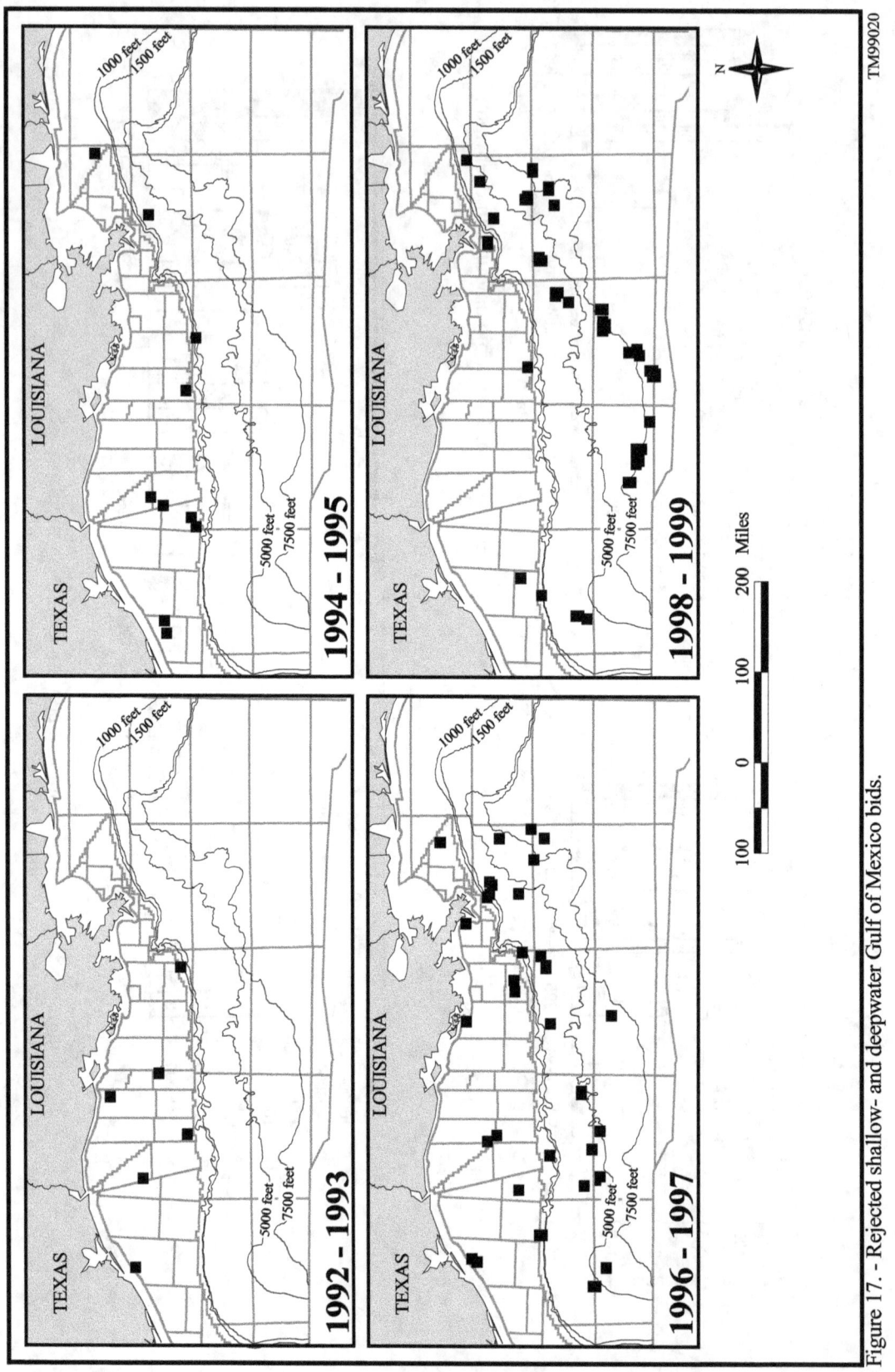

Figure 17. - Rejected shallow- and deepwater Gulf of Mexico bids.

24

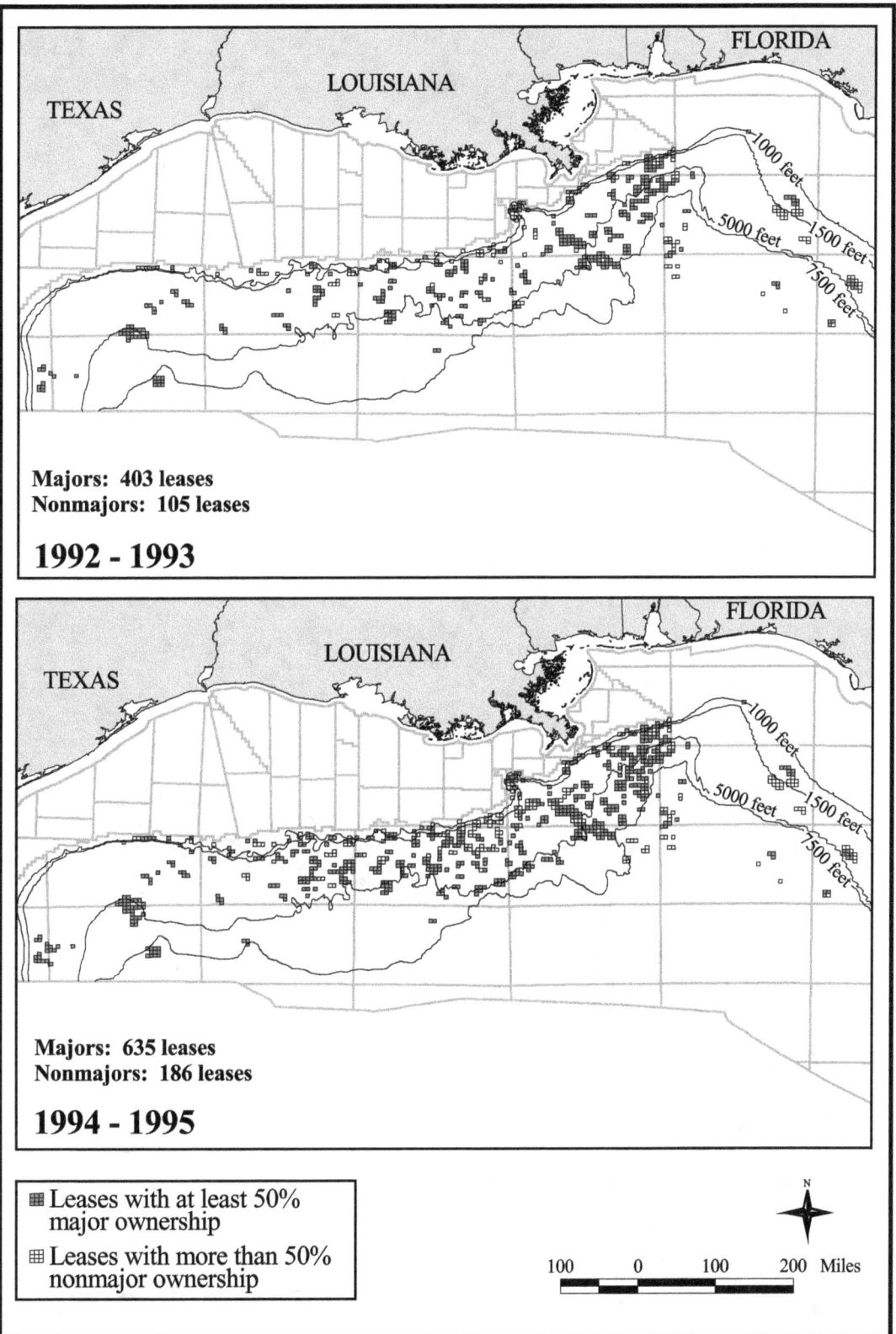

Figure 18. - Ownership of deepwater leases.

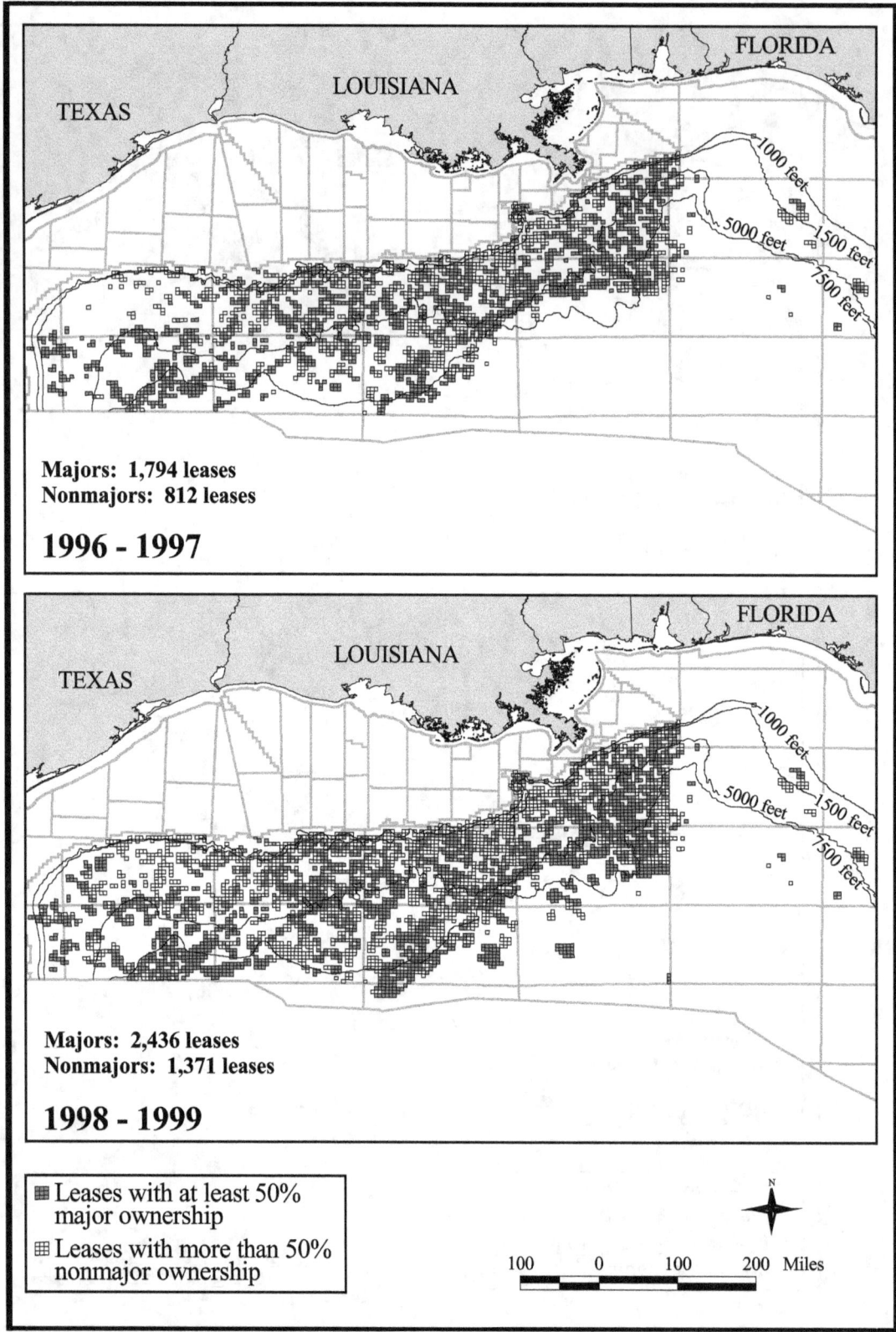

Figure18. - *continued* - Ownership of deepwater leases.

HG99009

production size. It is merely a convenient category for the purpose of comparison.) Figure 18 illustrates the relative lease-holding positions of majors versus nonmajors. Leases with a majority ownership by majors are dark gray, and those majority-owned by nonmajors are white with a black outline. Note that majors dominated deepwater leasing in 1992 and 1993. In 1994 and 1995, majors still dominated leasing in the deepest waters, leading the charge into this frontier. In 1996 nonmajors began acquiring significant lease holdings, a trend that continued to grow through 1999.

The type of companies active in deepwater clearly changed with the increased presence of nonmajor oil and gas companies. Another change in deepwater lease ownership came with the recent wave of company mega-mergers. Figure 19 shows the impact on lease holdings caused by several recent mergers and probable future mergers. These mergers increase the diversity of lease holdings for the merged companies. For example, BP focused heavily on the deepwater GOM, whereas Amoco was mixed between deep- and shallow water, and Arco focused on shallow water. The potential combination of companies yields a large GOM leasehold in all water depths and geographic areas. (As of this writing, the BP Amoco merger with Arco is not yet approved.)

Since the deepwater arena is already heavily leased, the number of leases that are relinquished or expire will influence activity in future lease sales. Since most companies can only drill a small percentage of their active leases, potentially high-quality leases often expire without being tested. The turnover of these leases often results in re-leasing at higher prices, "farm outs" to nonmajors, opportunities for nonmajors to gain a lease position and, potentially, more rapid exploration and development of the acreage.

Figure 20 shows leases that will expire in the coming years, assuming each lease expires at the end of its primary lease term (without a lease term extension). Note that lease terms vary according to water depth. Primary lease terms are 5 years in length for blocks in less than 400 meters of water, 8 years in length for blocks in 400-799 meters of water, and 10 years in length for blocks in 800 meters of water or greater. Therefore, in the absence of primary lease term extensions, all currently active shallow water leases will expire before 2005 (thus the sparse population and absence of expiring shallow water leases in certain frames of figure 20). The upcoming lease sales in 2000 and 2001 will offer a large number of expiring deepwater leases. The 2002 and 2003 lease sales will offer only a handful of expiring deepwater leases because of depressed leasing activity in 1992 and 1993. Deepwater lease availability should increase again in 2004 and 2005 and, beginning in 2006, numerous deepwater leases will become available, this latter resulting from the leasing boom that began in 1996. These lease expiration projections will put pressure on leaseholders to drill and evaluate their holdings and provide opportunities for other companies to enter an active play by acquiring leases as they expire or obtaining "farm-outs" from companies with excess acreage.

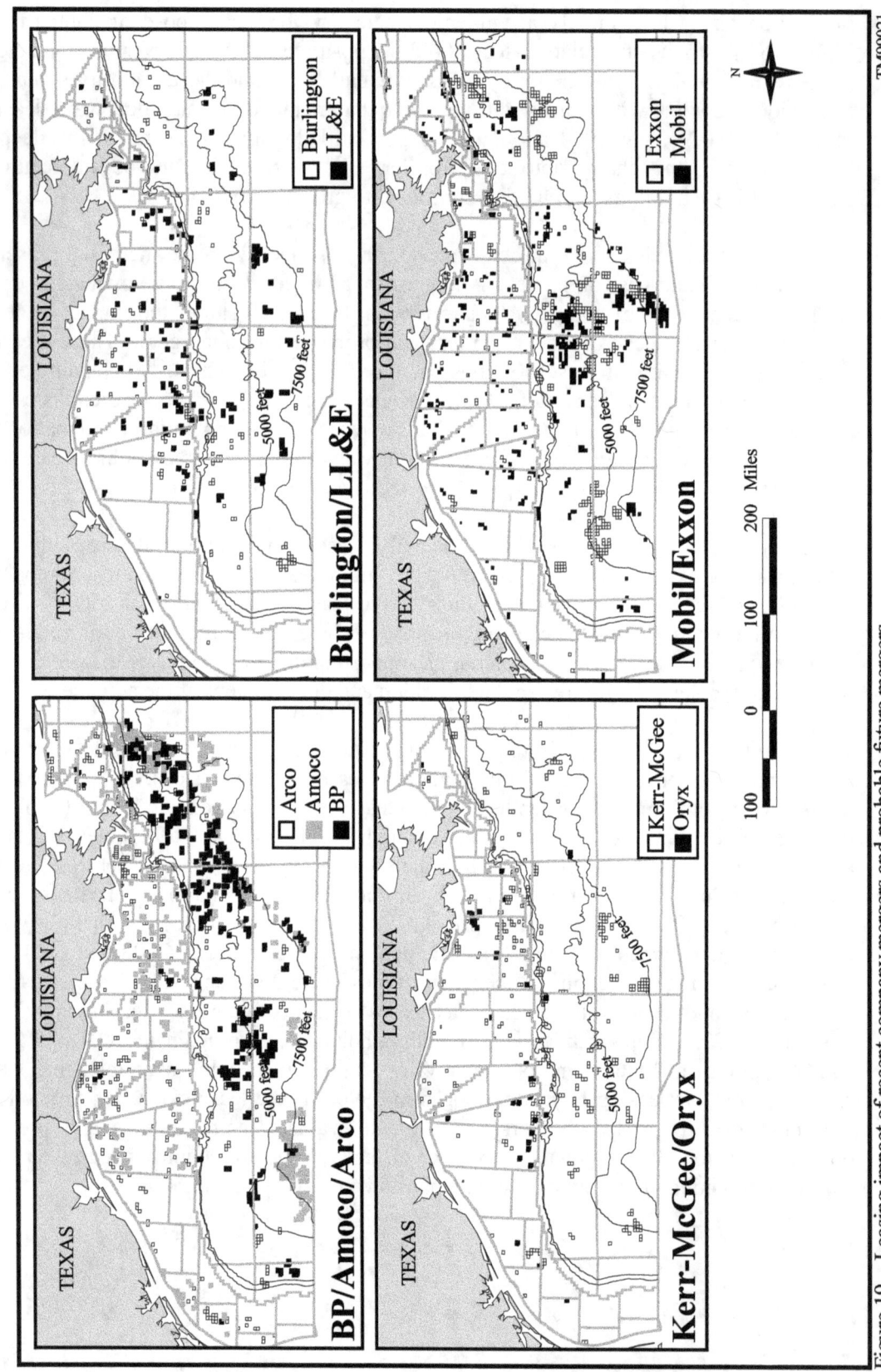

Figure 19. - Leasing impact of recent company mergers and probable future mergers.

28

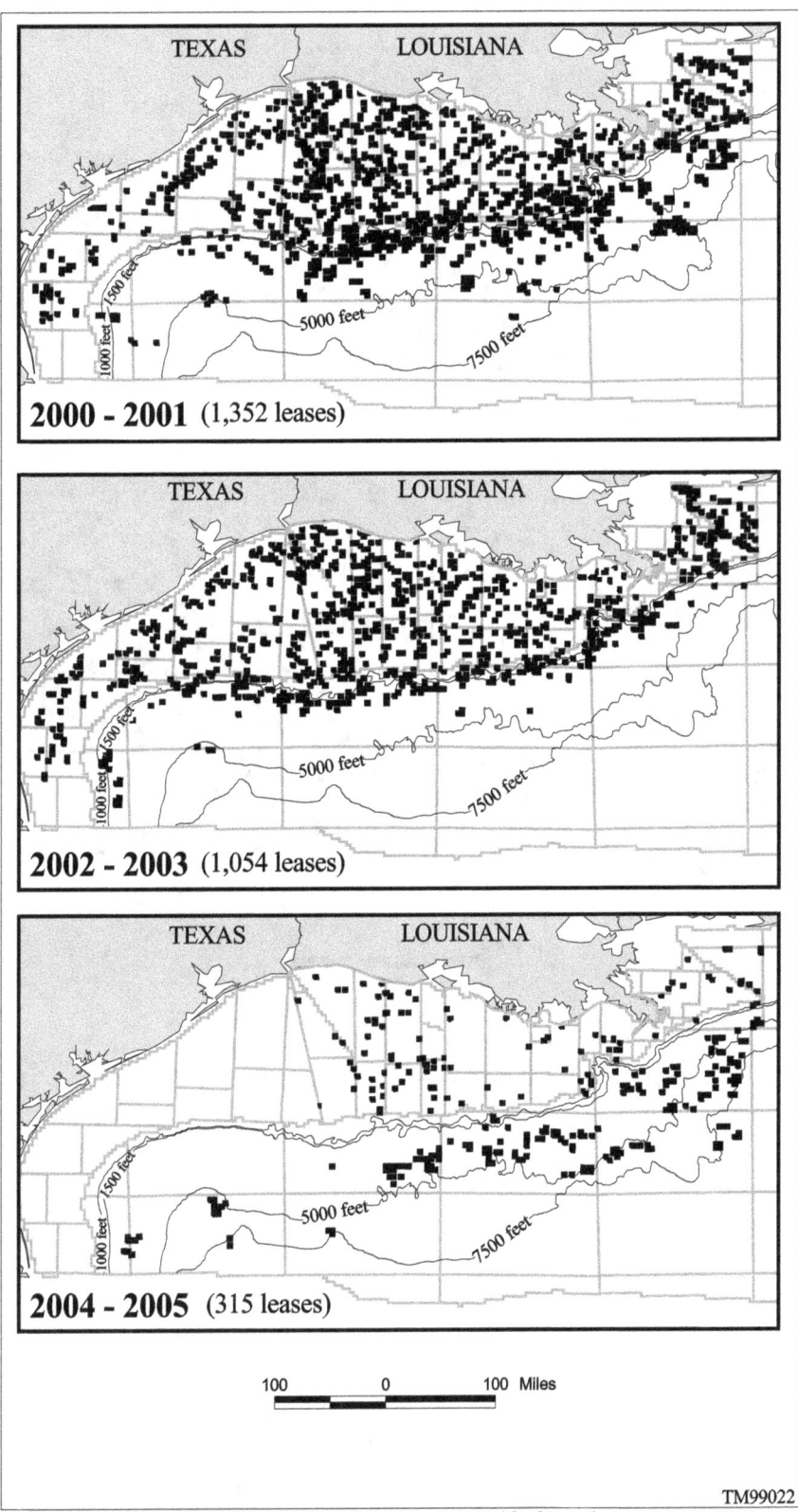

Figure 20. - Anticipated lease expirations in the Gulf of Mexico.

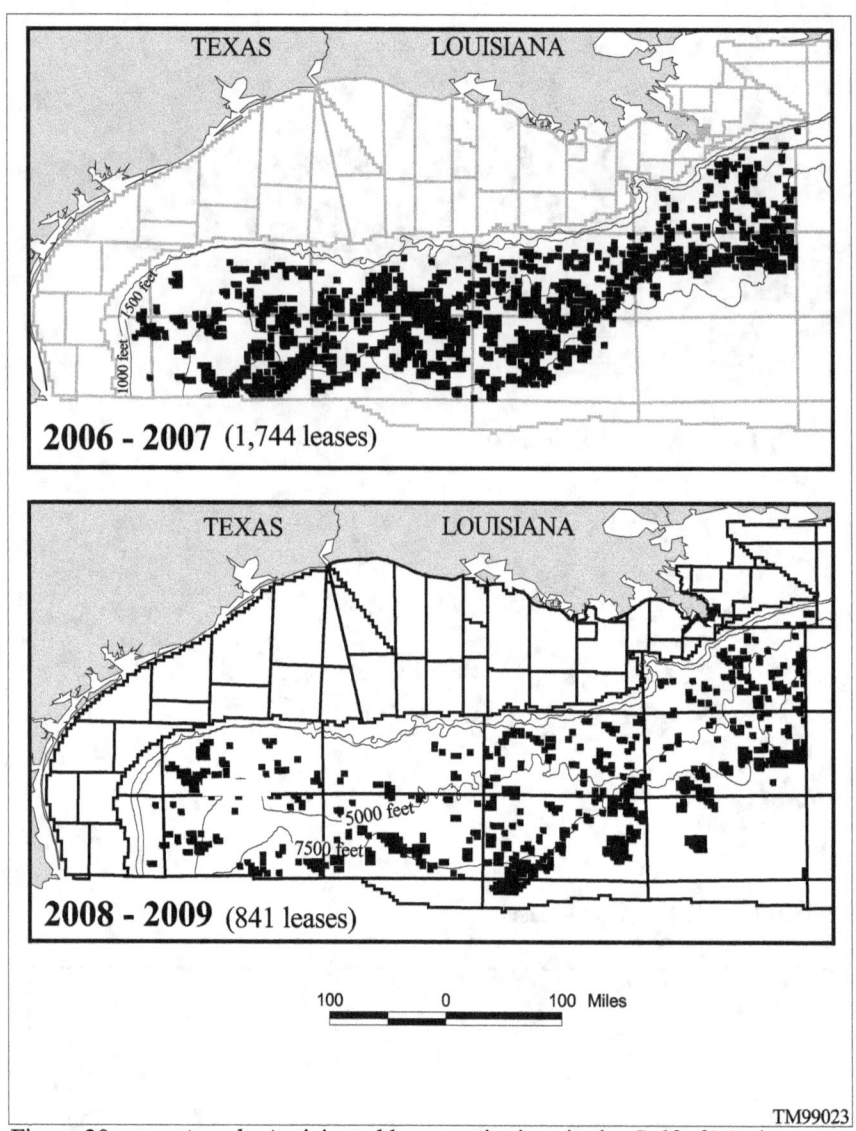

Figure 20. - *continued* - Anticipated lease expirations in the Gulf of Mexico.

Drilling and Development

Although there are numerous deepwater leases and prospects waiting to be drilled, there are a limited number of deepwater drilling rigs available. Figure 21 shows the average number of rigs drilling in the deepwater GOM since 1992. There has been a steady increase in deepwater rig activity during this time, and the number of rigs drilling in the deepwater GOM is expected to continue increasing slightly through 2001 (DeLuca, 1999; Harding, 1999). Even with the increased number of deepwater rigs, only a small fraction of the 3,670 active deepwater leases can be drilled before they expire.

Figure 22 shows the approximate number of deepwater GOM rigs and their water depth capabilities. Currently, there are about 45 rigs in the GOM capable of drilling deepwater wells (DeLuca, 1999; Harding, 1999; Kelly, 1999; Bollinger, 1999; Rig Census, 1999; Gulf of Mexico Weekly Rig Locator, 1999). Five of these rigs can drill in water depths up to 1,499 ft; about 22 rigs have a maximum water depth capacity between 1,500 and 4,999 ft; 14 rigs are capable of drilling in 5,000 to 7,499 ft of water; and only 4 GOM rigs can drill in greater than or equal to 7,500 ft of water. The fact that the number of available GOM rigs (figure 22) is slightly higher than the average number drilling (figure 21) is not because of inactive deepwater rigs. It probably reflects rigs changing locations and rigs drilling in water depths less than their maximum capabilities.

Currently, there are only four rigs in the GOM capable of drilling in water depths of 7,500 ft or greater and, thus, the evaluation of the 470 active leases in this water depth range will be constrained. However, there are approximately 15 rigs under construction that can drill in these ultra-deep waters (DeLuca, 1999; Harding, 1999; Rig Census, 1999; Hart's E&P Magazine, 1999; Bollinger, 1999; Kelly, 1999). There is a worldwide demand for these ultra-deepwater rigs, and economics play a significant role in their migration to and from oil regions. Several ultra-deepwater rigs have left the GOM in favor of international locations (particularly West Africa), although other deepwater rigs (with more limited water depth capabilities) have moved into the GOM. Unfortunately, very few deepwater rigs are under construction for deliveries beyond 2000 (DeLuca, 1999).

Figure 23 illustrates a significant increase in the number of deepwater exploratory wells drilled from 1992 through 1998, especially in the 1,500-4,999 ft water depth range. Exploratory drilling in 1999 was down slightly from the record 1998 levels and, thus far, there has been minimal drilling activity in water depths greater than 7,500 ft. Figure 25 illustrates the geographic distribution of deepwater exploratory wells. Note the progression into the western GOM and into deeper water through time. (Note also that we define exploratory wells as those numbered 1 thru 5. For example, the GC 136 No. 7 well is classified as exploratory, but we define it as a development well in this report because it probably had a developmental objective.)

Figure 24 shows increased development drilling from 1992 through 1997. The vast majority of development drilling was in the 1,500-4,999 ft water depth range. Note also the diminished deepwater development drilling in 1998 and 1999. Figure 26 depicts the

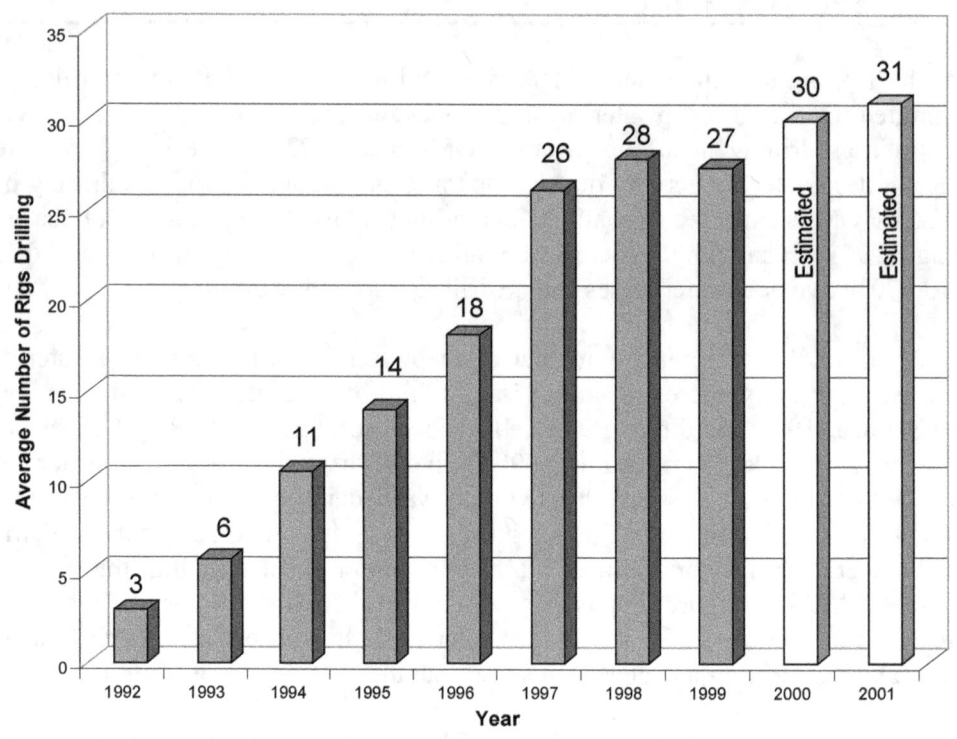

Figure 21. - Average number of rigs drilling in the deepwater Gulf of Mexico.

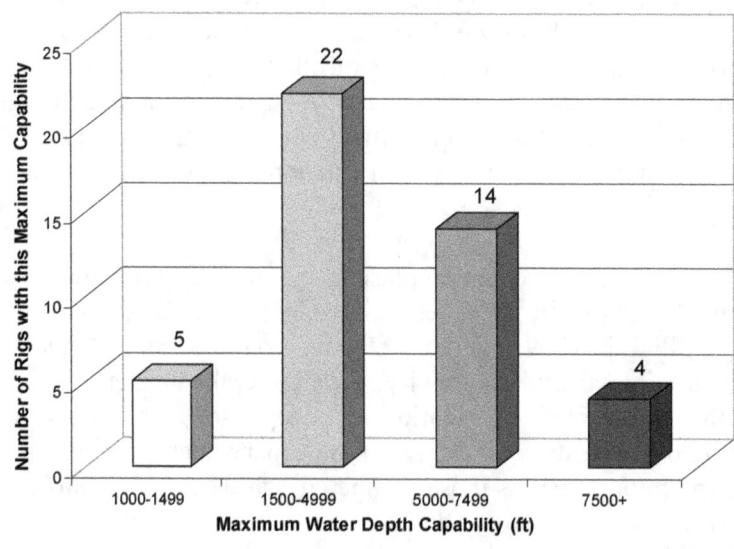

Figure 22. - Approximate number of deepwater Gulf of Mexico rigs subdivided according to their maximum water depth capabilities.

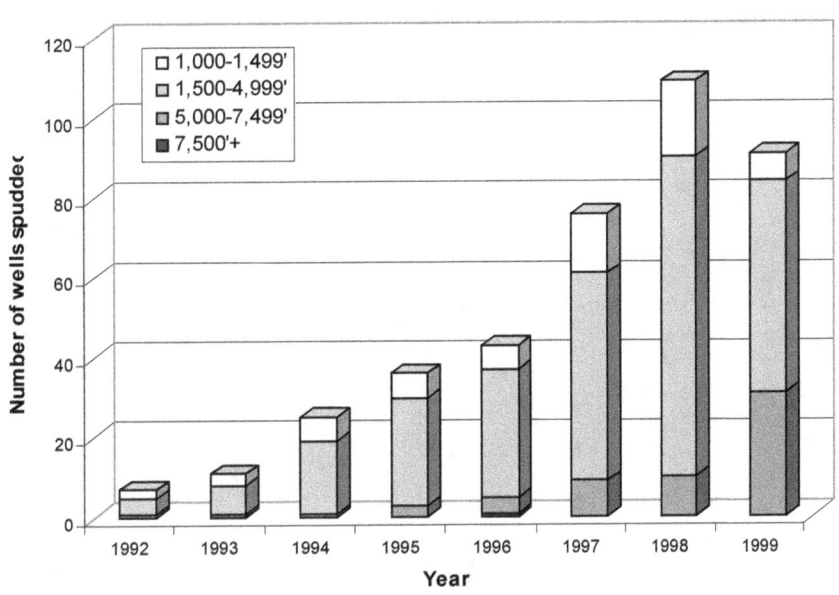

Figure 23. - Deepwater exploratory wells drilled in the Gulf of Mexico, subdivided by water depth.

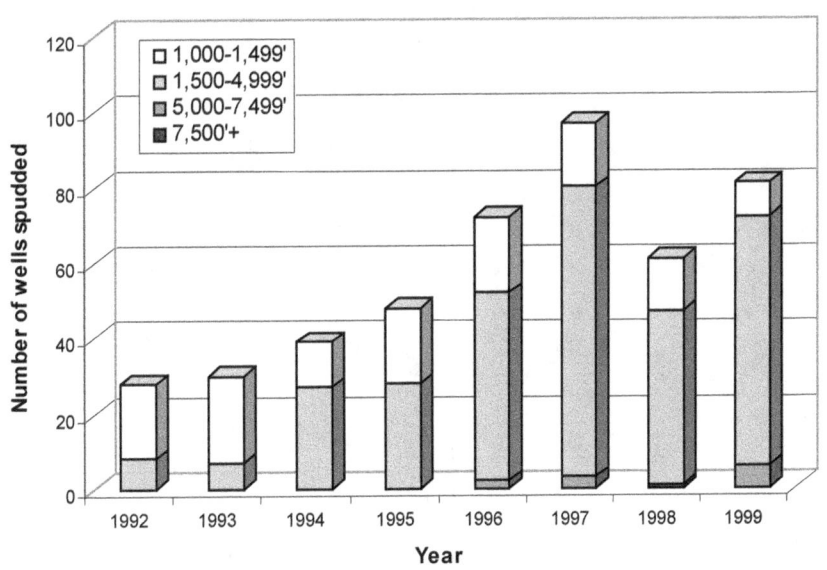

Figure 24. - Deepwater development wells drilled in the Gulf of Mexico, subdivided by water depth.

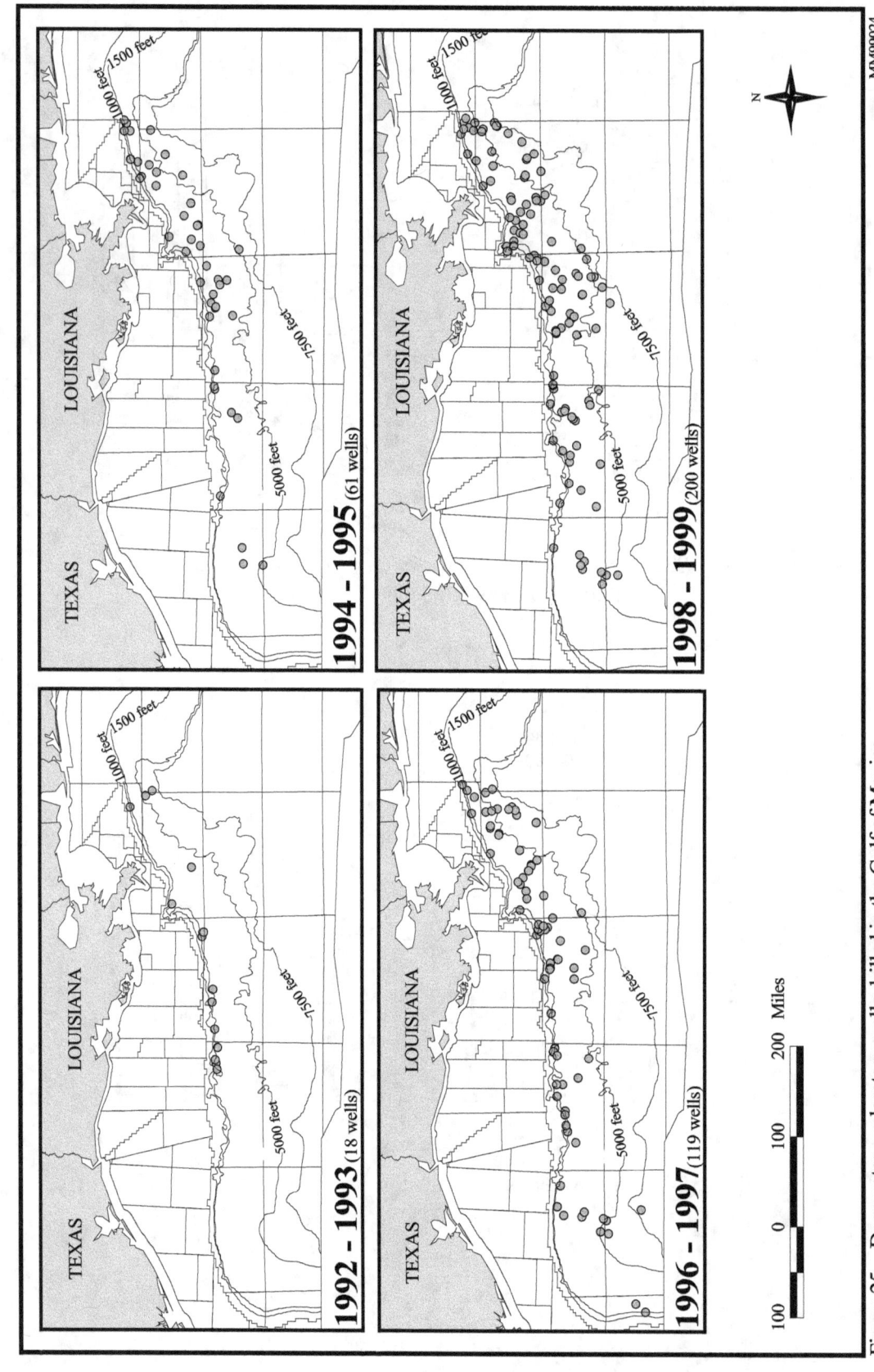

Figure 25. - Deepwater exploratory wells drilled in the Gulf of Mexico.

34

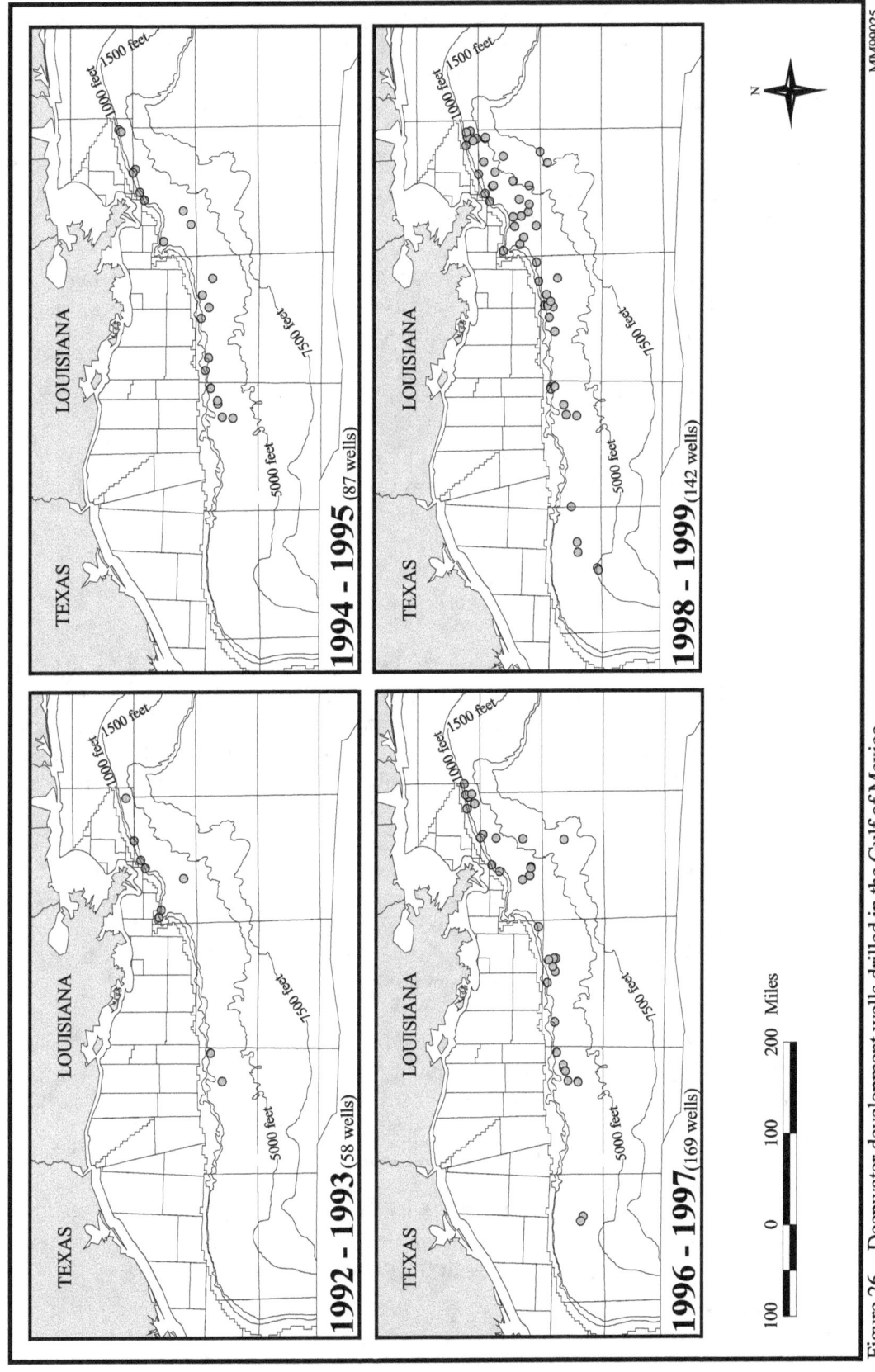

Figure 26. - Deepwater development wells drilled in the Gulf of Mexico.

35

locations of these development wells. Once again the data reveal a general increase in activity with time as well as a trend toward increasing water depth with time.

When deepwater exploratory and development GOM drilling are combined, it becomes clear that deepwater drilling increased rapidly from 1992 to 1997, but remained flat from 1997 through 1999. That is, 170 to 175 deepwater wells were drilled each year (from 1997 through 1999), even though the focus shifted between exploration and development. This trend mirrors the deepwater rig activity (figure 21), as expected.

Other indicators of deepwater activity include the number of plans received and approved by MMS. Although the order of plan submission and drilling activities can vary with projects, operators generally proceed as follows:

- file a Plan of Exploration (POE),
- drill exploratory wells,
- file a conceptual Deep Water Operations Plan (DWOP),
- file a Development Operations Coordination Document (DOCD),
- drill development wells,
- file a preliminary DWOP,
- file a final DWOP, then
- begin production.

Figure 27 shows the number of deepwater POE's, deepwater DOCD's, and DWOP's received each year since 1992 (DWOP's were not required until 1995). Some shallow-water activities are included in the DWOP data because DWOP's must be filed and approved for developments in greater than 1,000-ft water depths and all subsea developments regardless of water depth. Further, figure 27 shows the years when the initial (conceptual) DWOP's were filed for each project.

There was a sharp increase in deepwater exploratory plan approvals from 1992 through 1999. The number of deepwater development plan approvals also showed a general increase during this time. The number of DWOP's filed was relatively constant from 1996 through 1999, with the exception of 1997. Recall that 1997 was also a year when an exceptionally high number of development wells were drilled (figure 24).

Figures 28 and 29 show the progression of GOM drilling toward deeper wells and greater water depths. Figure 28 shows the maximum true vertical depth (TVD) of wells drilled each year since 1947 (when drilling in the Gulf of Mexico OCS began). Clearly, there was a gradual increase in maximum TVD from 13,636 ft in 1948 to 26,978 ft in 1998. Figure 29 shows the maximum water depth drilled each year since 1947. Deepwater drilling began in 1974 (1,024 ft), followed by significant water depth milestones in 1976 (1,986 ft), 1984 (3,534 ft), and 1987 (7,500 ft). The current record (7,716 ft) is likely to be eclipsed soon; an operator filed plans to drill in over 9,600 ft of water by yearend 2000. Unlike the gradual progression of TVD through time, the progression into deep water was very rapid.

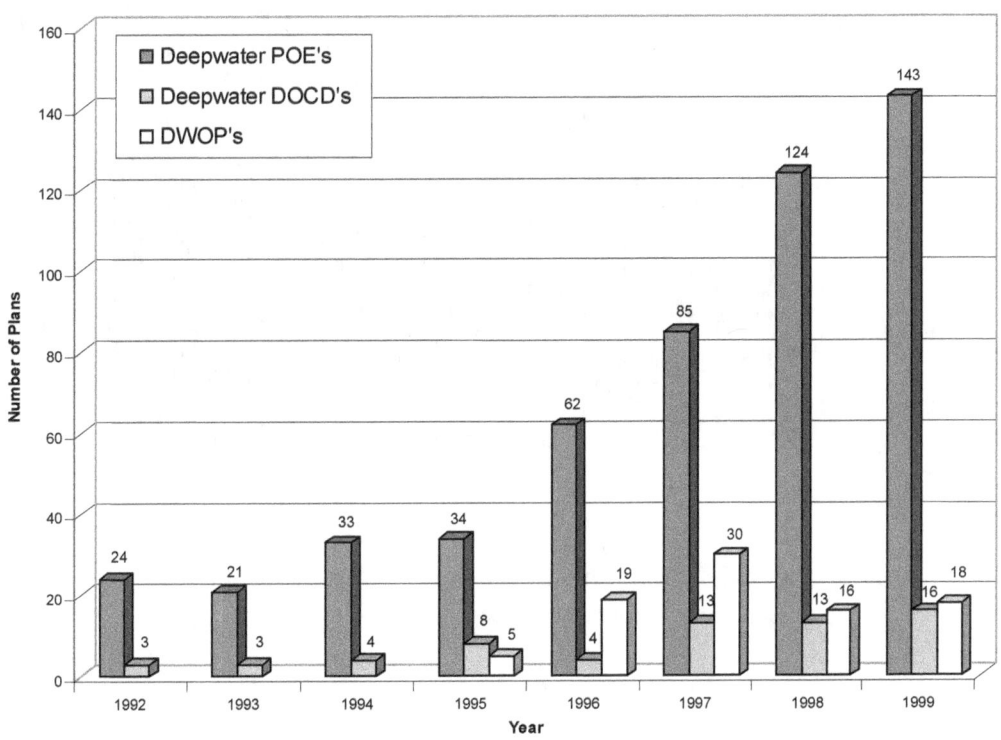

Figure 27. - Deepwater POE's approved, deepwater DOCD's approved, and DWOP's received in the Gulf of Mexico since 1992.

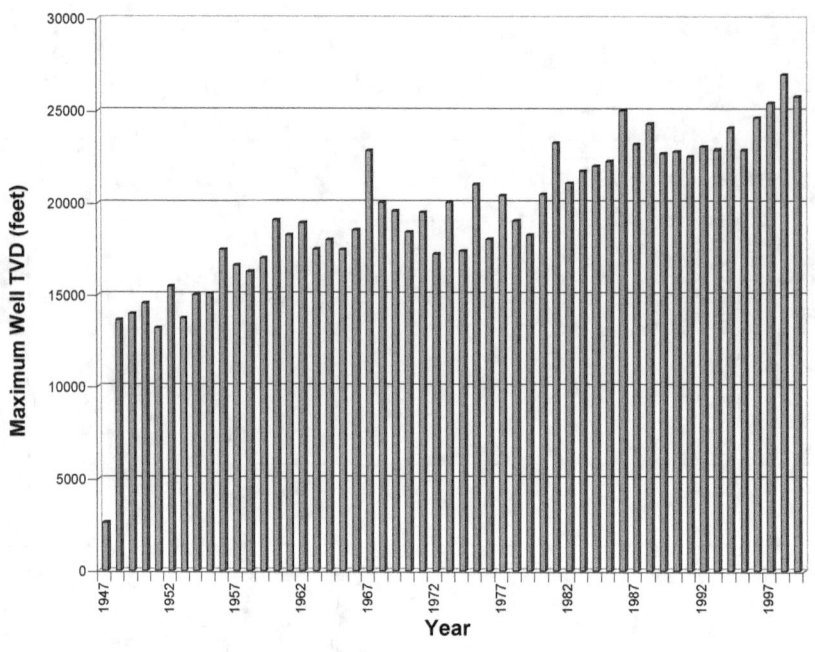

Figure 28. - Maximum wellbore true vertical depth (TVD) drilled each year.

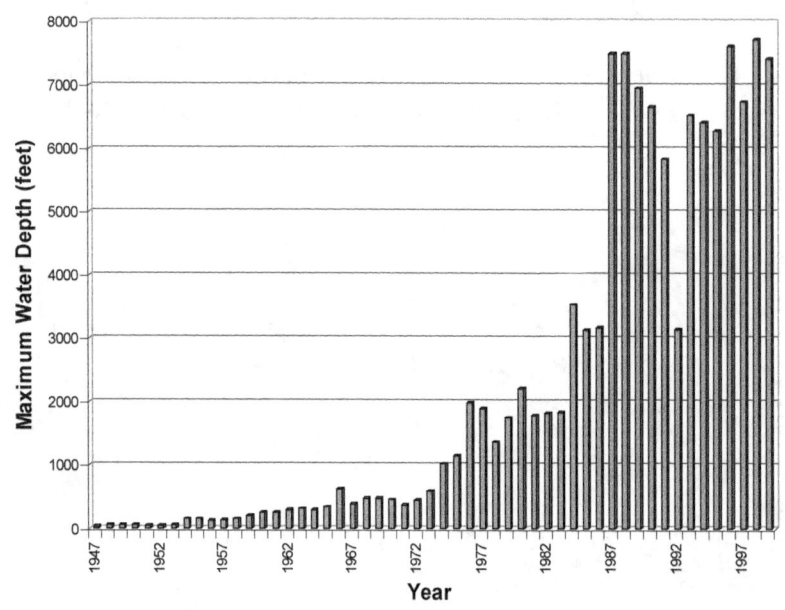

Figure 29. - Maximum water depth drilled each year.

There are several development systems capable of producing deepwater oil and gas. Figure 30 illustrates several systems that are currently available and table 1 lists the systems used to develop productive deepwater GOM fields. Fixed platforms (e.g., Cognac) have economic water depth limits of about 1,200 to 1,500 ft. Compliant towers (e.g., Baldpate) may be considered for water depths of approximately 1,000 to 3,000 ft. Tension leg platforms (TLP's) and mini-TLP's (e.g., Auger and Morpeth, respectively) are frequently used in 1,000 to 5,000-ft water depths. Spars (e.g., Genesis) and other floating production systems may be used in 8,000-ft water depths and beyond. Subsea systems (e.g., Mensa) are also capable of producing hydrocarbons from reservoirs in excess of 8,000-ft water depths. Though no floating, storage, production, and offloading system (FPSO) has been installed in the Gulf of Mexico, strong interest has been expressed by several companies to use this type of production facility. Water depth ranges expected for FPSO's range from 1,000 to greater than 8,000 ft.

The FPSO technology and shuttle tankering of OCS crude oil present many new operational options and questions. The FPSO systems can be used as crude processing facilities or for storing large volumes of crude oil (1 million barrels or more) in the hull prior to offloading and tankering to shore. The MMS is preparing an environmental impact statement (EIS) to assess the potential impacts of FPSO operations and associated support activities within the Central and Western Planning Areas of the GOM. A contract to prepare the EIS was awarded to Ecology and Environment, Inc. in April 1999. It is anticipated that completion of the EIS will occur in late 2000. The MMS's objectives in preparing the EIS are listed below.

- To ensure that FPSO operations and associated support operations conducted in the deepwater Gulf of Mexico OCS occur in a technically safe and environmentally sound manner;
- To describe the types and ranges of potential FPSO operations and associated support activities;
- To determine reasonable alternatives to specific aspects of proposed FPSO operations;
- To identify potential impacts from FPSO operations and associated support activities on the marine, coastal, and human environments;
- To evaluate the significance of potential impacts from FPSO operations and associated support activities;
- To develop appropriate measures to mitigate potentially significant impacts from FPSO operations and associated support activities; and
- To provide a National Environmental Policy Act (NEPA) summary document that will support future NEPA assessments of FPSO operations and associated support activities.

Subsea systems are a key component to the recent increase in deepwater activity. These systems are generally multicomponent seafloor facilities that allow for the production of hydrocarbons in water depths that would normally preclude installing conventional fixed or bottom-founded platforms. Through an array of subsea wells, manifolds, central umbilicals, and flowlines, a subsea system can be located many miles away in deeper

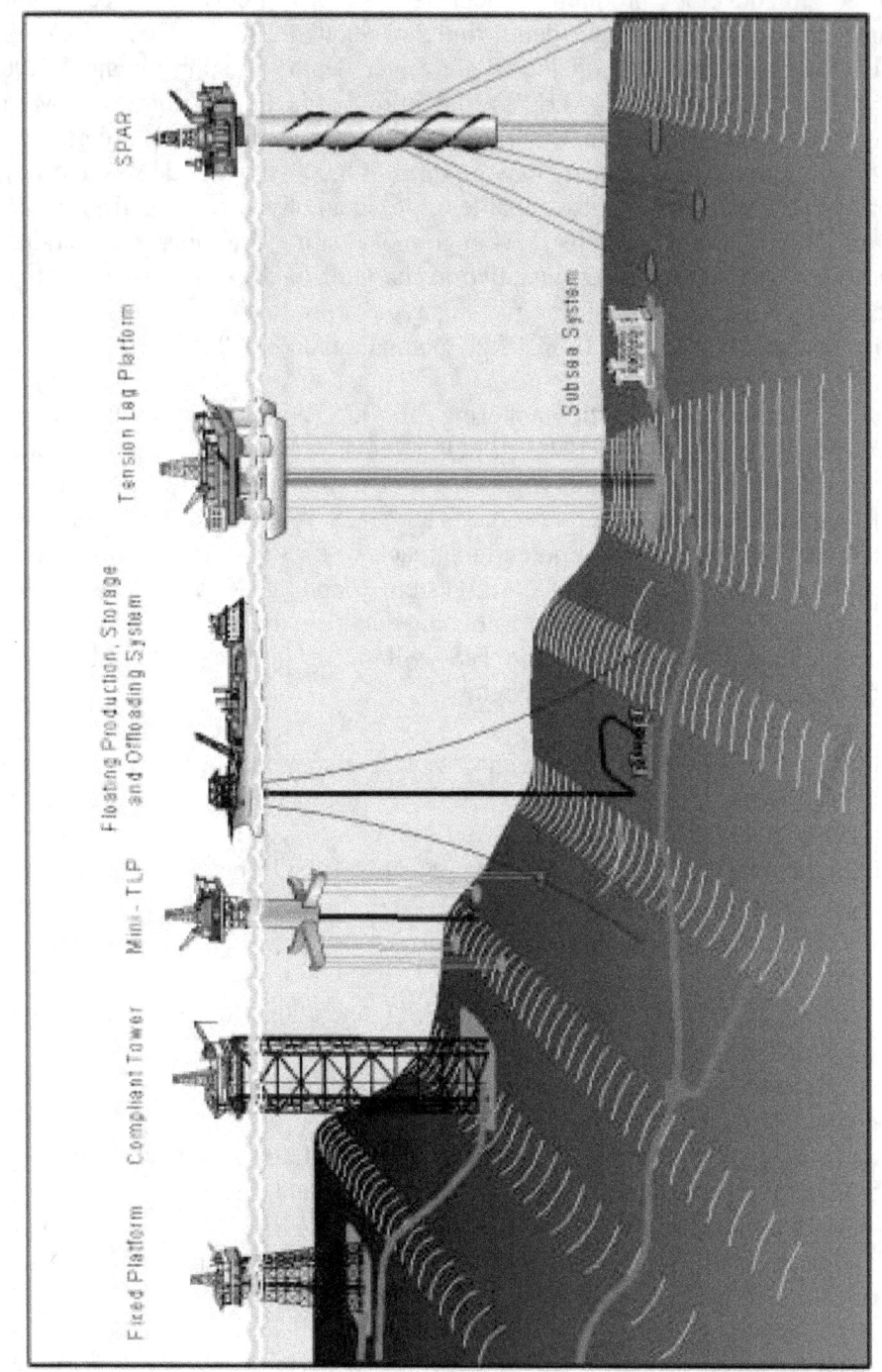

Figure 30. - Deepwater development systems.

40

Table 1. - Development Systems of Productive Deepwater GOM Fields.

Year of First Production	System Type	Field Nickname	Block	Water Depth	Operator
1979	Fixed Platform	Cognac	MC 194	1,023 ft	Shell Offshore Inc.
1984	Compliant Tower	Lena	MC 281	1,017 ft	Exxon
1988*	FPS	Unnamed	GC 75	2,172 ft	Oryx
1988*	Semi-Submersible	Unnamed	GC 29	1,554 ft	Placid
1989	Fixed Platform	Bullwinkle	GC 65	1,330 ft	Shell Offshore Inc.
1989	TLP	Jolliet	GC 184	1,722 ft	Conoco
1991	Fixed Platform	AmberJack	MC 109	1,058 ft	BP Amoco
1993*	Subsea	Diamond	MC 445	2,095 ft	Oryx
1993*	FPS/Subsea	Seattle Slew	EW 914	1,019 ft	Tatham
1993	Subsea	Zinc	MC 354	1,478 ft	Exxon
1994	Fixed Platform/Subsea	Pompano/Pompano II	VK 990	1,445 ft	BP Amoco
1994	Subsea	Tahoe/Tahoe II	VK 783	1,492 ft	Shell Deepwater Prod. Inc.
1994	TLP	Auger	GB 426	2,864 ft	Shell Deepwater Prod. Inc.
1995*	Semi-Submersible	Cooper	GB 387	2,163 ft	EEX
1995	Subsea	Unnamed	VK 862	1,043 ft	Walter Oil & Gas
1996	Subsea	Popeye	GC 116	2,067 ft	Shell Deepwater Prod. Inc.
1996	Subsea	Rocky	GC 110	1,621 ft	Shell Deepwater Prod. Inc.
1996	TLP/Subsea	Mars	MC 807	2,958 ft	Shell Deepwater Prod. Inc.
1997	Spar	Neptune/Thor	VK 825	1,866 ft	Kerr-McGee
1997	Subsea	Mensa	MC 731	5,330 ft	Shell Deepwater Prod. Inc.
1997	Subsea	Troika	GC 244	2,681 ft	BP Amoco
1997	TLP	Ram Powell	VK 956	3,247 ft	Shell Deepwater Prod. Inc.
1998	Compliant Tower	Baldpate	GB 260	1,605 ft	Amerada Hess
1998	Mini-TLP/Subsea	Morpeth/Klamath	EW 921	1,706 ft	British-Borneo
1998	Subsea	Salsa	GB 171	1,074 ft	Shell Offshore Inc.
1998	Subsea	Arnold	EW 963	1,752 ft	Marathon
1999	Mini-TLP/Subsea	Allegheny	GC 254	3,186 ft	British-Borneo
1999	Spar	Genesis	GC 205	2,599 ft	Chevron
1999	TLP	Ursa	MC 810	3,885 ft	Shell Deepwater Prod. Inc.
1999	Subsea	Angus	GC 112	1,465 ft	Shell Deepwater Dev. Inc.
1999	Subsea	Dulcimer	GB 367	1,124 ft	Mariner
1999	Subsea	Gemini	MC 292	3,745 ft	Texaco
1999	Subsea	Macaroni	GB 602	3,600 ft	Shell Deepwater Dev. Inc.
1999	Subsea	Unnamed	EW 1006	1,832 ft	Walter Oil & Gas
1999	Fixed Platform	Virgo	VK 823	1,154 ft	Elf

* Indicates fields that are no longer on production.

water and tied back to existing "host" facilities in shallow water. Figure 31 shows the number of subsea completions each year since 1955 (only productive wells were counted). There were fewer than five subsea completions per year until 1989. This number increased dramatically throughout the 1990's.

The technology required to implement subsea production systems in deepwater evolved significantly in the last decade. This evolution is apparent in figure 32, which shows the deepest subsea completion was in 350 ft of water until 1988, when the water depth record jumped to 2,243 ft (GC 75 field). In 1996 another milestone was reached with a subsea completion in 2,956 ft of water (Mars field), followed by a 1997 subsea completion in 5,295 ft of water (Mensa field). A listing of productive subsea completions in the GOM OCS can be found in Appendix C.

According to MMS records, there is a total of 186 subsea completions to date, 83 of which (45%) were completed in the four years 1996-1999. Of the 186 subsea completions, 62 of these (33%) were in deepwater and 40 (65%) of these deepwater subsea completions occurred from 1996 through 1999. Figure 33 shows that the number of deepwater subsea completions increased steadily from 1994 through 1999, with anomalously high numbers of deepwater completions in 1993 and 1996. The use of subsea completions in shallow water also increased rapidly from 1992 through 1997. There was a significant drop in the number of shallow-water subsea completions in 1998, possibly related to low oil prices.

The distance from subsea completions to their host facilities varies considerably. Figure 34 shows the lengths of deepwater flowlines that are 4 to 12 inches in diameter and carry bulk oil or gas (pipeline segments less than 1,000 ft long are excluded). The majority of these flowlines are less than 15 miles long. A few tiebacks are 20 to 30 miles, and Shell's Mensa field is a record 62 miles from its host facility in West Delta Block 143. Most of these pipelines were approved after 1992, but there is no clear relationship between approval date and length of tieback.

The pipeline infrastructure to bring deepwater oil and gas onshore also expanded during the 1990's. Figures 35a and 35b show a significant increase in the mileage of deepwater pipelines approved the past few years. A significant portion of this increase involved pipelines less than or equal to 12 inches in diameter (figure 35a), and an exponential increase occurred in the mileage of large (greater than 12 inches in diameter) deepwater oil and gas pipelines laid over the past 3 years (figure 35b).

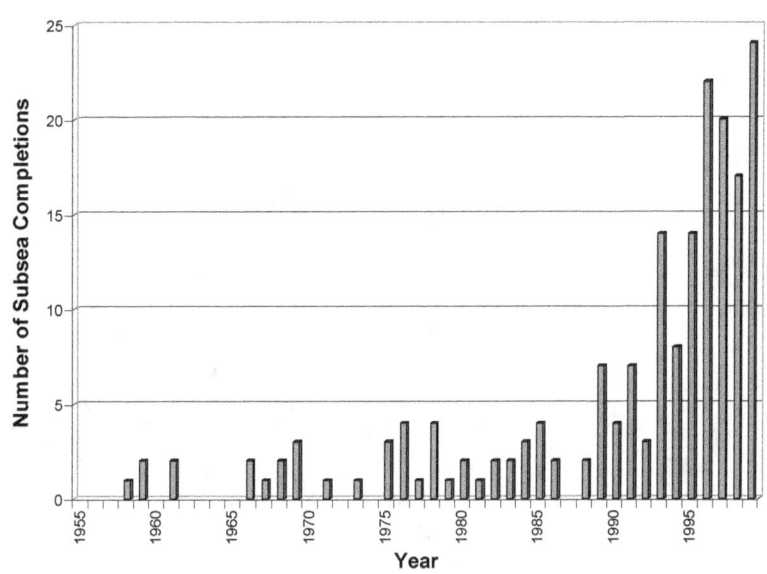

Figure 31. - Number of subsea completions each year.

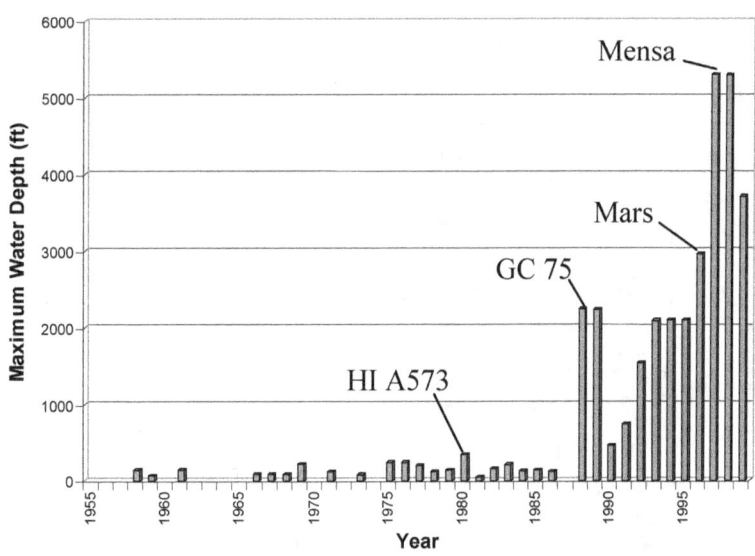

Figure 32. - Maximum water depths of subsea completions each year.

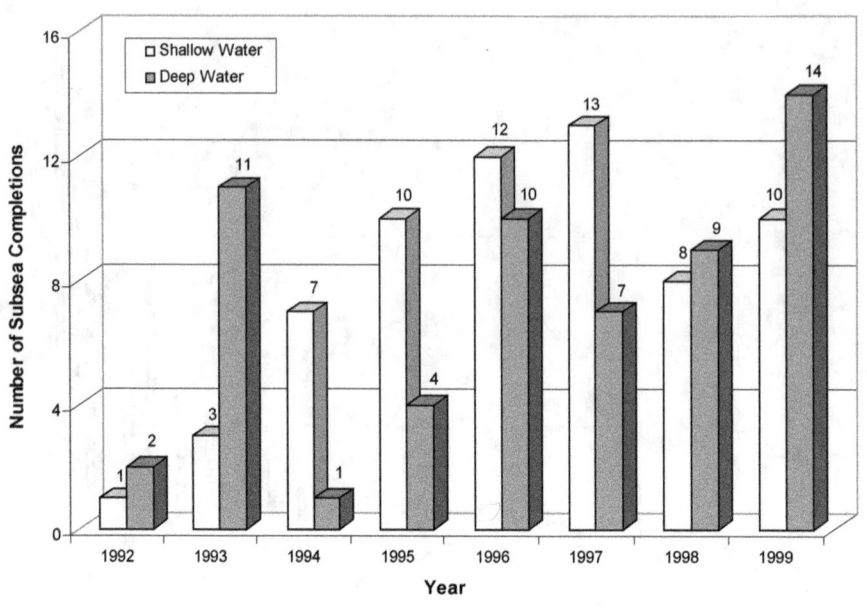

Figure 33. - Number of shallow- and deepwater subsea completions each year since 1992.

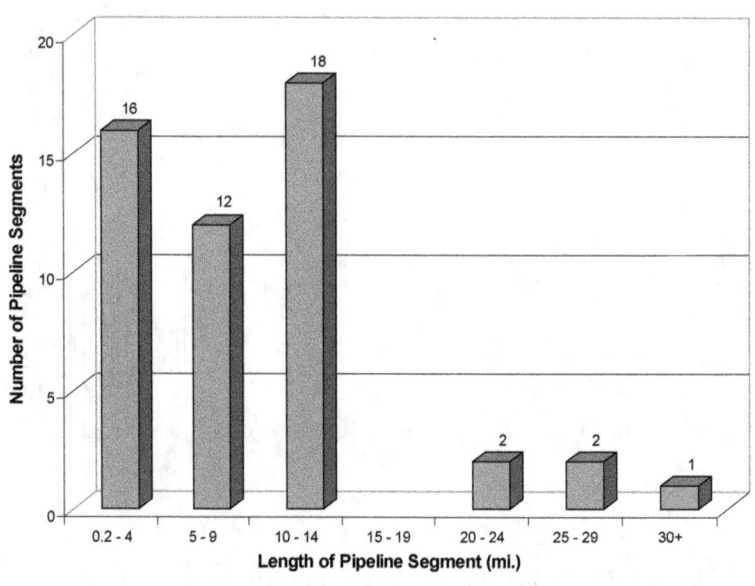

Figure 34. - Length of subsea tiebacks.

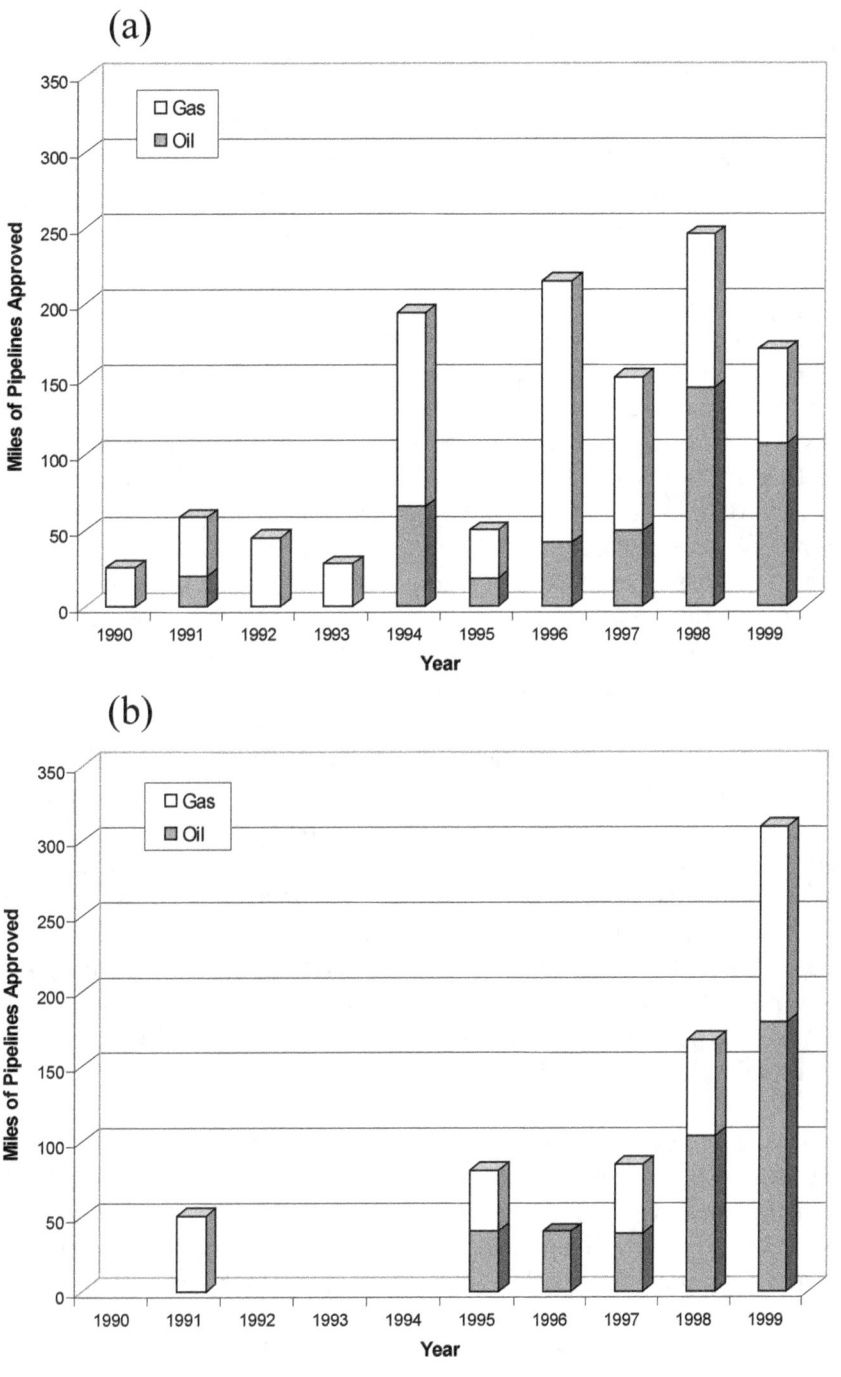

Figure 35. - Deepwater oil and gas pipelines (a) less than or equal to 12 inches in diameter and (b) greater than 12 inches in diameter.

Reserves and Production

The deepwater GOM has contributed major additions to the total region's reserves. Figure 36a shows the proved reserves added each year by water depth category. Additions from the shallow waters of the GOM declined in recent years but, beginning in 1975, the deepwater area started contributing significant new reserves.

There is often a significant time lag between a successful exploratory well and its hydrocarbons reaching proved status (in a producing or soon to be producing field). The success of an exploratory well may remain concealed from the public for several years until an operator requests a "Determination of Well Producibility" from MMS. A successful MMS determination then "qualifies" the lease as producible and the discovery is placed in a field by MMS. The discovery date of that field is then defined as the TD (total depth) date of the field's first well that encountered significant hydrocarbons. Hydrocarbon reserves are still considered unproved until it is clear that the field will go on production. Then the reserves move into MMS's proved category. Figure 36b includes both proved and unproved reserves for each water depth category. This figure shows declining reserve additions in shallow water similar to figure 36a, but reveals significantly more deepwater reserve additions.

The most important feature of the deepwater field discoveries is observed in figure 36c, where the average size of deepwater fields is many times larger than the average size of shallow-water fields. During the 1990's the average shallow-water field added approximately 5 MMBOE of proved and unproved reserves. In contrast, the average deepwater field during this same period added over 47 MMBOE of proved and unproved reserves (over 9 times more than shallow water). In the most active deepwater exploration area, water depths between 1,500 and 7,499 ft, the average deepwater field contributed over 60 MMBOE (12 times more than the average shallow-water field addition). This is typical of frontier areas and indicates that there are many large deepwater fields yet to be discovered.

Figure 37 shows the number of deepwater fields discovered each year, according to MMS criteria, since 1975. (See appendix A for a listing of deepwater fields and discoveries.) The number of field discoveries for any given year is usually greater than the number of fields that actually go on production. The difference between the number of field discoveries and the number of those that actually produce climbs in the late 1990's, since these recent field discoveries have had little time to reach production. Because of this time lag between exploratory drilling and first production, the true impact of recent, large deepwater exploratory successes are not yet reflected in MMS proved and unproved reserve estimates.

In an attempt to capture the impact these successful deepwater exploratory successes, figure 38 adds MMS known resource estimates and several industry-announced discoveries to the proved and unproved reserve volumes. The industry-announced discovery volumes contain considerable uncertainty, are based on limited drilling, include

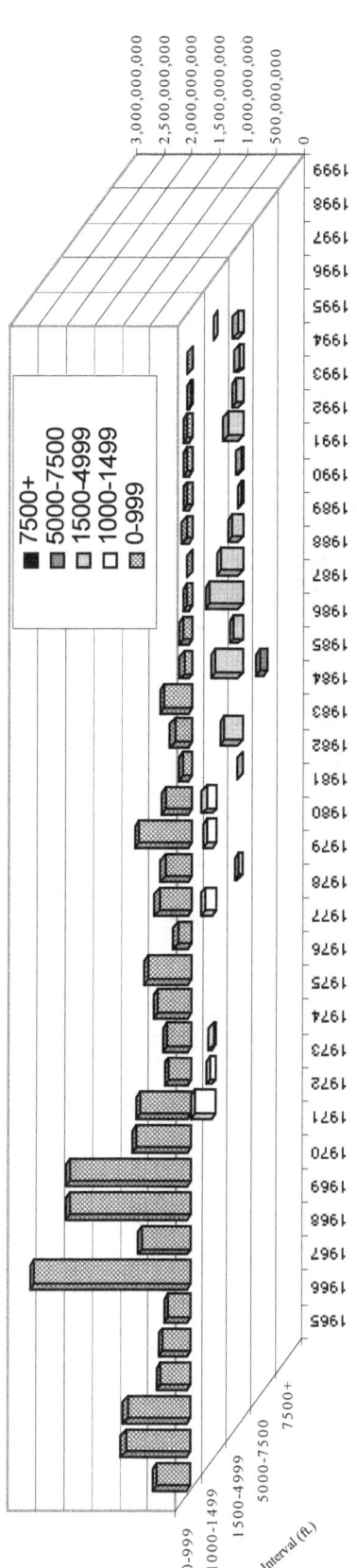

Figure 36a. - Proved reserve additions

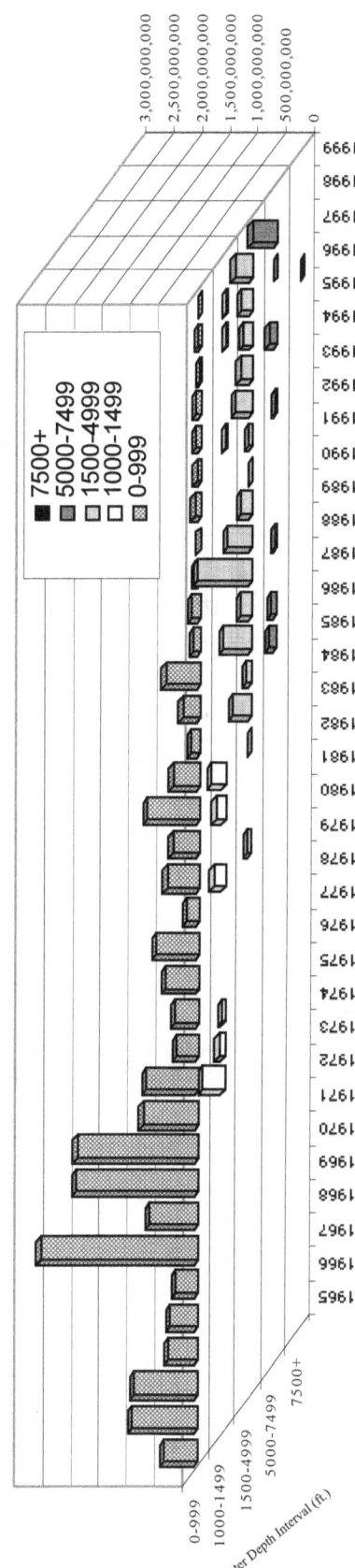

Figure 36b. - Proved and unproved reserve additions

47

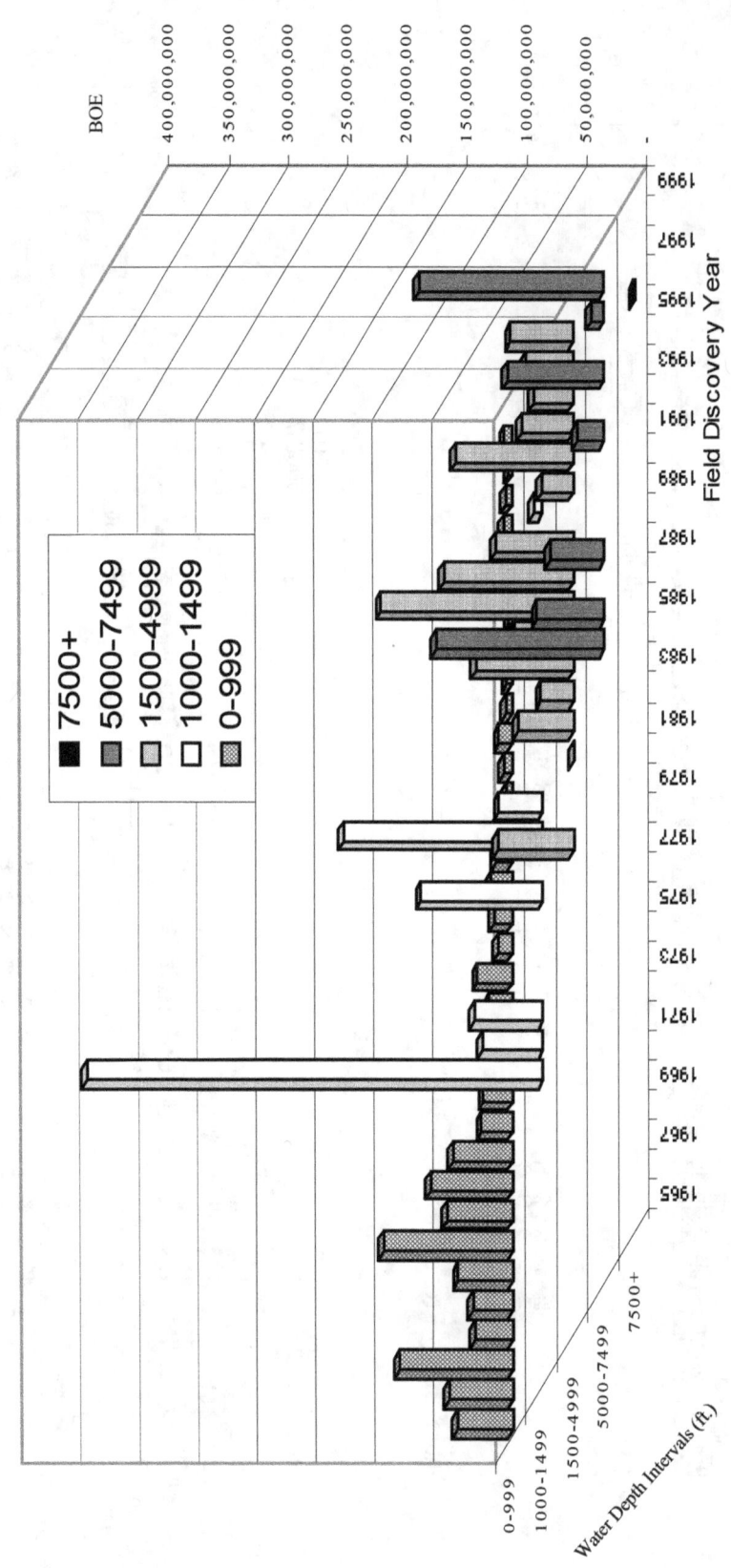

Figure 36c. - Average field size using proved and unproved reserves.

48

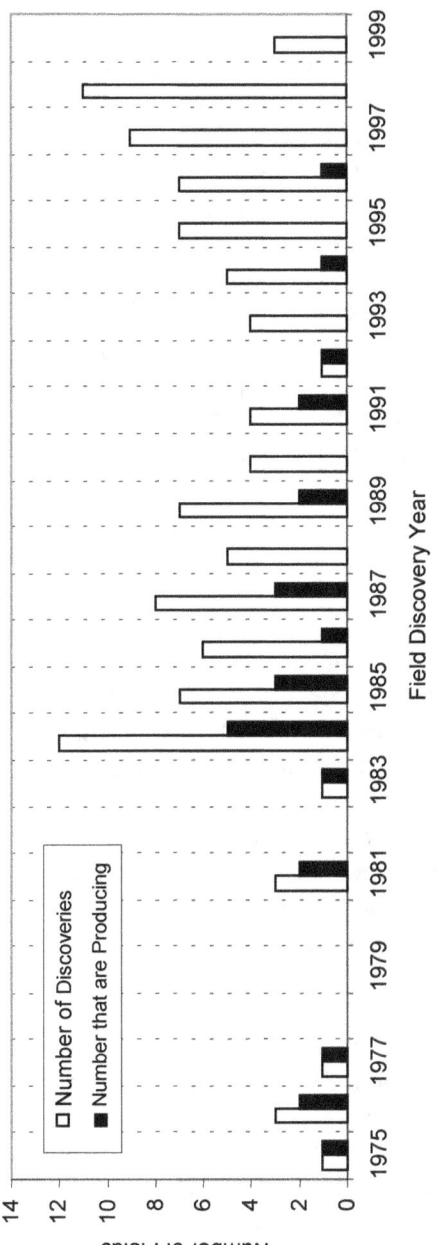

Figure 37. - Number of deepwater field discoveries and resulting number of producing fields.

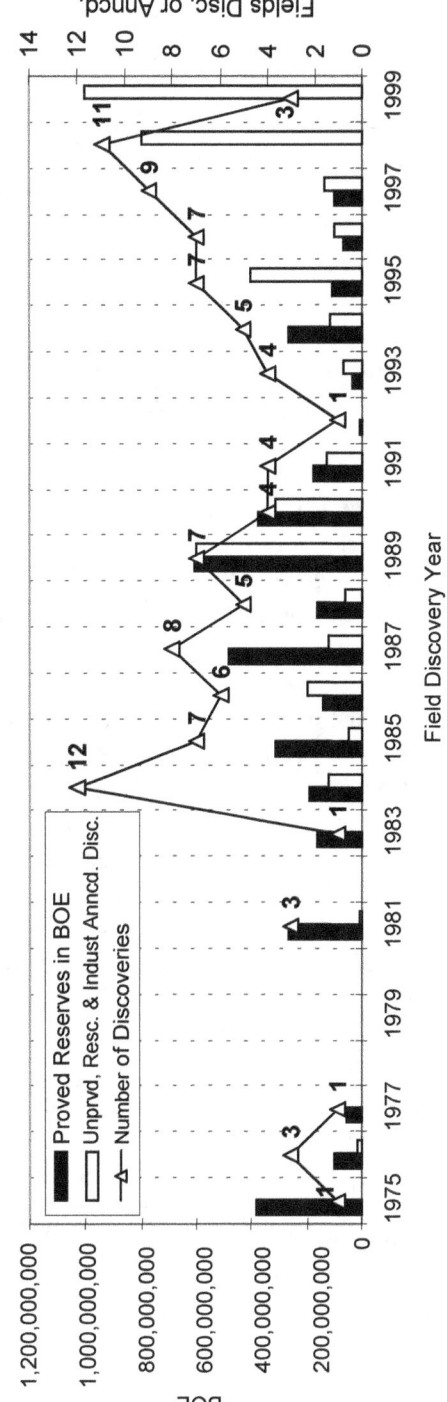

Figure 38. - Number of deepwater field discoveries and new hydrocarbons found (MMS reserves, MMS resources, and industry-announced discoveries).

49

numerous assumptions, and have not been confirmed by independent MMS analyses. They do, however, illustrate recent activity better than using only MMS proved reserve numbers. In figure 38, the apparent decline of proved reserve additions in recent years is caused by the previously mentioned developmental time lag.

The inclusion of the very large, recent, industry-announced deepwater discoveries with MMS resource estimates illustrates that successful deepwater exploration is adding significant volumes to total GOM hydrocarbon reserves. These large additions show the excellent potential for continued future growth in deepwater activity levels and deepwater reserves. Figure 39 illustrates the distribution of new hydrocarbon additions in the GOM categorized by water depth. When compared with figures 36a (proved reserves) and 36b (proved and unproved reserves), figure 39 (proved reserves, unproved reserves, known resources, and industry-announced reserves) shows that recently announced industry discoveries will add significant reserves to the GOM if industry estimates are accurate.

Seismic acquisition, leasing, bid rejects, drilling, and discoveries all stepped into deeper waters with time. The final piece in the puzzle, production, is no exception. Figure 40 illustrates the relative volume of production from each GOM lease through time. Notice the large deepwater volumes, which appear in 1998 and 1999. Lagging slightly behind the boom in exploratory activity, deepwater production is emerging quickly and impressively.

Figure 41a illustrates historic trends in oil production (Melancon and Baud, 2000). Shallow-water oil production has been relatively flat to slightly declining, but deepwater oil production increased dramatically. In late 1999, deepwater GOM oil surpassed shallow-water production for the first time in history. This strong increase in deepwater oil production more than offsets recent declines in shallow-water oil production. Figure 41b shows similar production trends for gas. Shallow-water gas production was relatively stable over the past 15 years, with a slight recent decline. The steady increase in deepwater gas production that occurred in the past few years offset the shallow-water decline. Deepwater oil and gas production is expected to continue increasing through at least 2002 (Melancon and Baud, 2000).

A significant portion of deepwater production comes from subsea completions. Figure 42a shows that very little deepwater oil production came from subsea completions until mid-1995. By the fall of 1996, about 20 percent of deepwater oil production came from subsea completions. There was a slight decline in deepwater oil production from subsea completions in 1997, but increasing production since that time. Deepwater gas production from subsea completions (figure 42b) shows a similar trend. No deepwater gas production came from subsea completions in early 1993, but subsea completions accounted for over 40 percent of deepwater GOM gas production by mid-1994. There was a slight decline in deepwater gas production from subsea completions in 1995, but increasing production since that time. Subsea completions currently account for about 25 percent of deepwater oil production and about 40 percent of deepwater gas production.

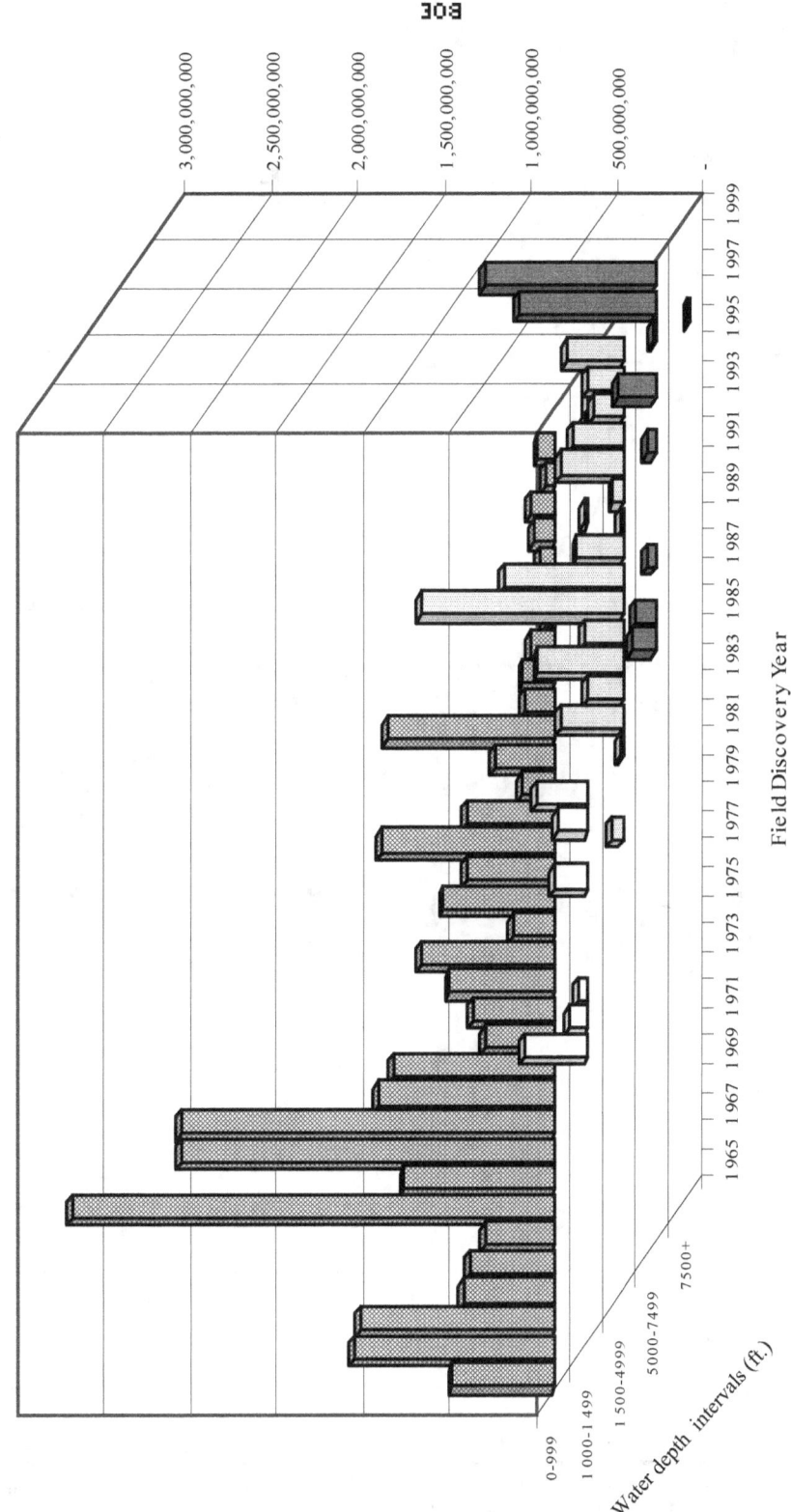

Figure 39. - BOE added (reserves, known resources, and industry-announced discoveries.)

51

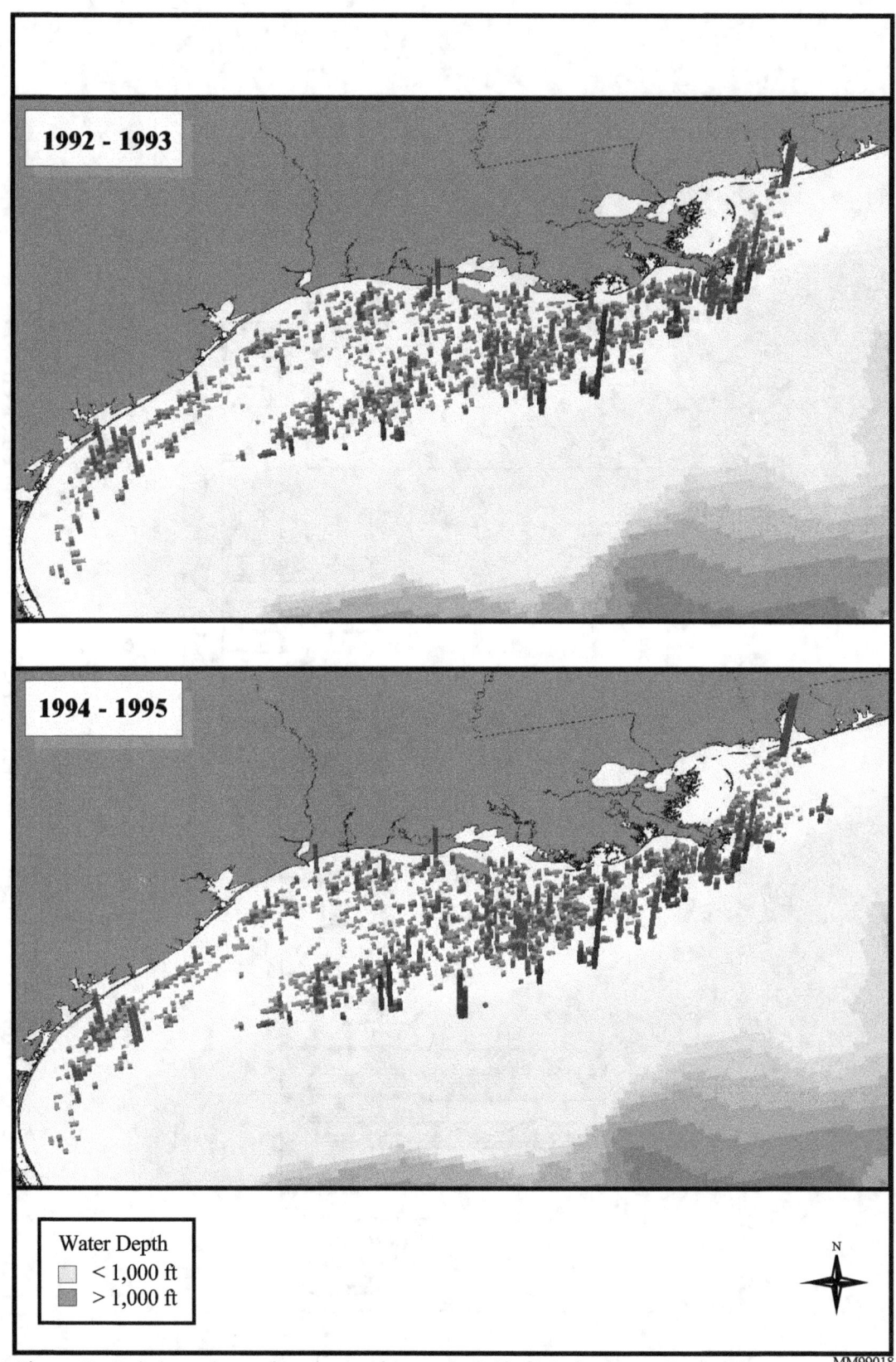

Figure 40. Relative volume of production from each Gulf of Mexico lease. Bar heights are proportional to total lease production (barrels of oil equivalent) during that time interval.

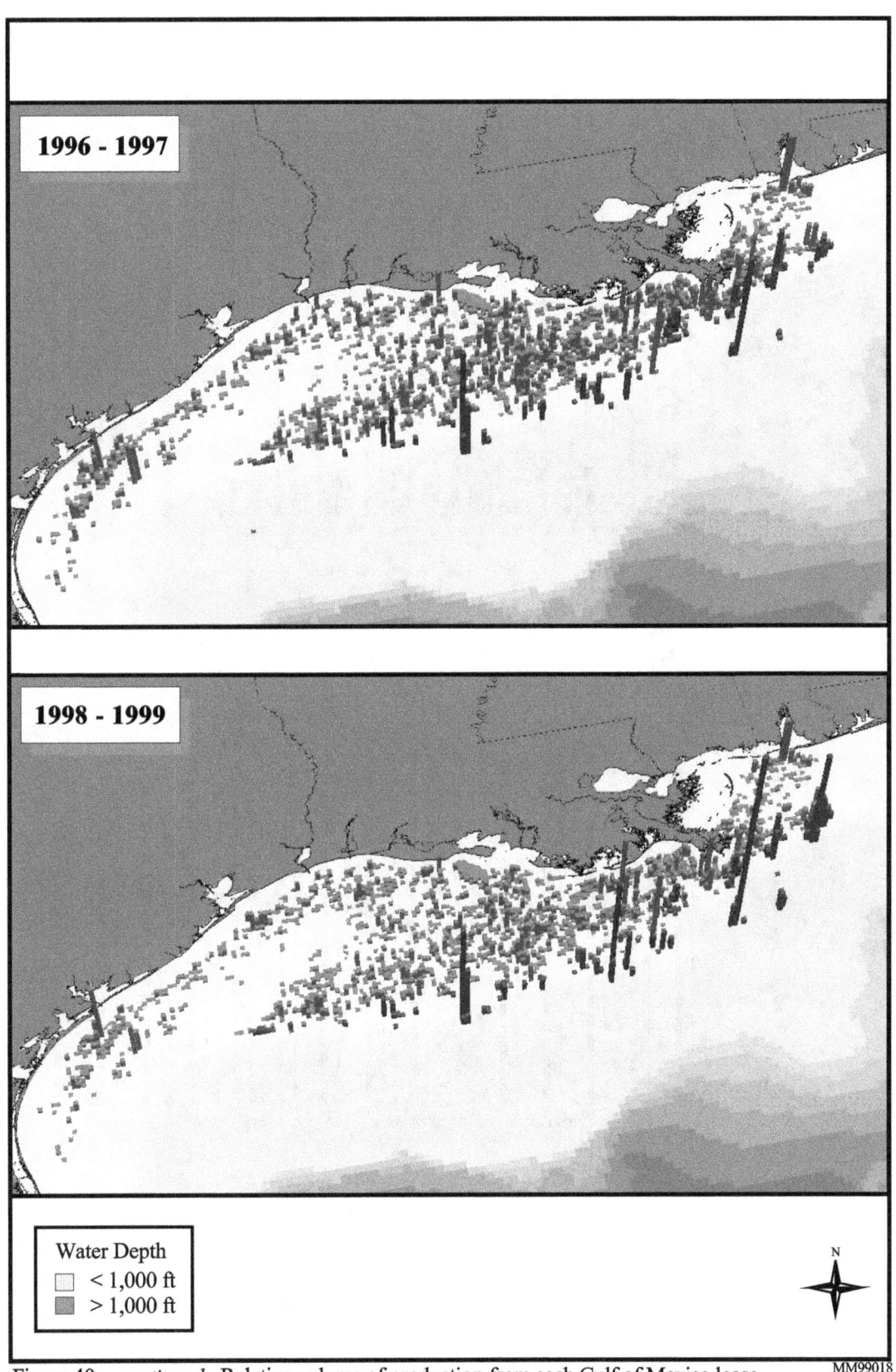

Figure 40. - *continued* - Relative volume of production from each Gulf of Mexico lease.
Bar heights are proportional to total lease production (barrels of oil equivalent) during that time interval.

(a)

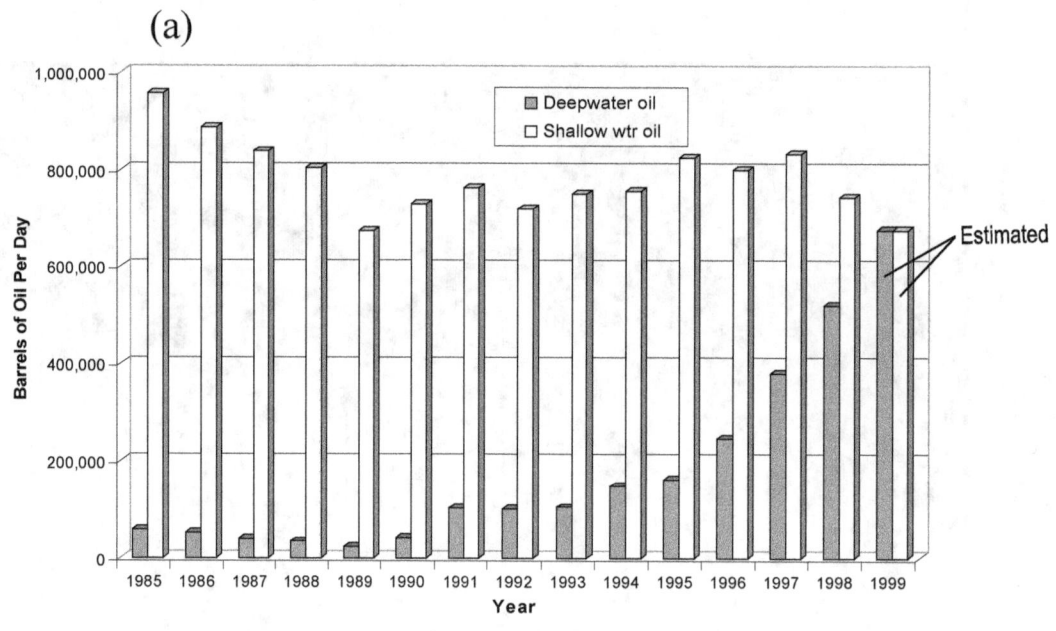

(b)

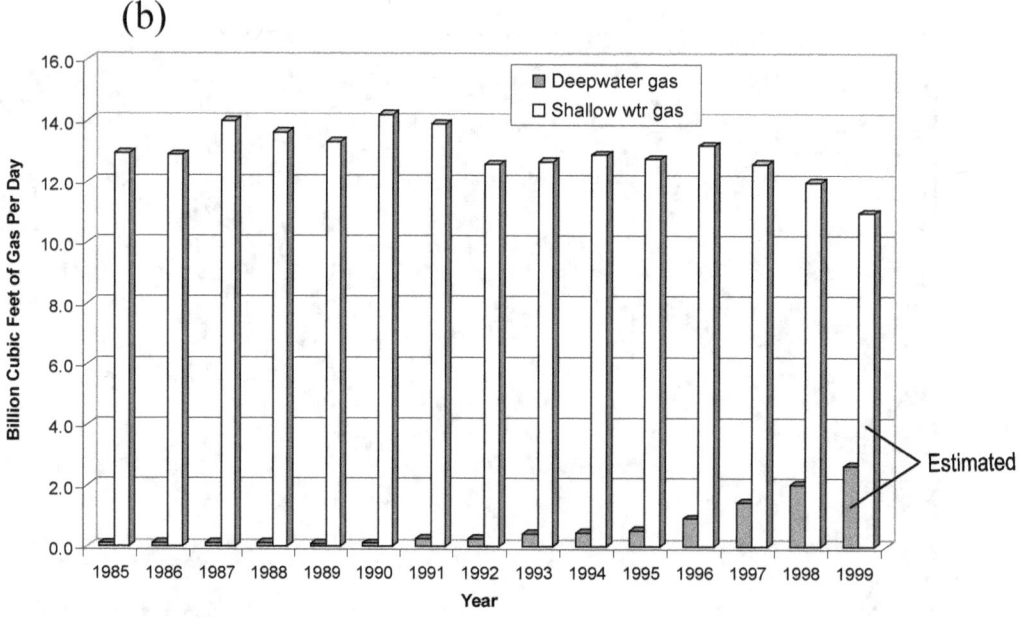

Figure 41. - Comparison of yearend shallow- and deepwater (a) oil production and (b) gas production.

54

(a)

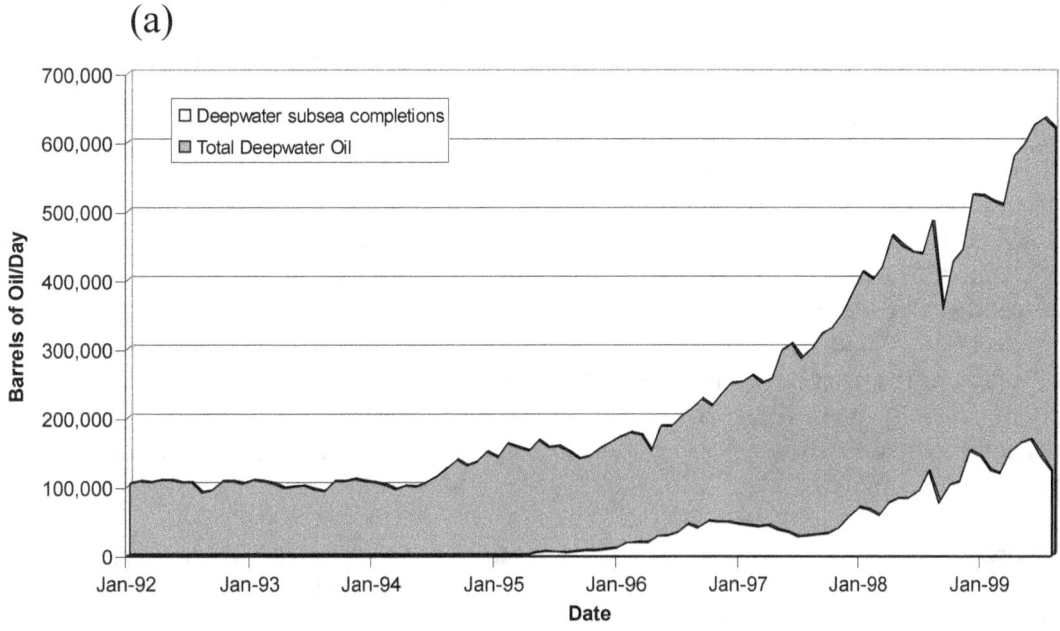

(b)

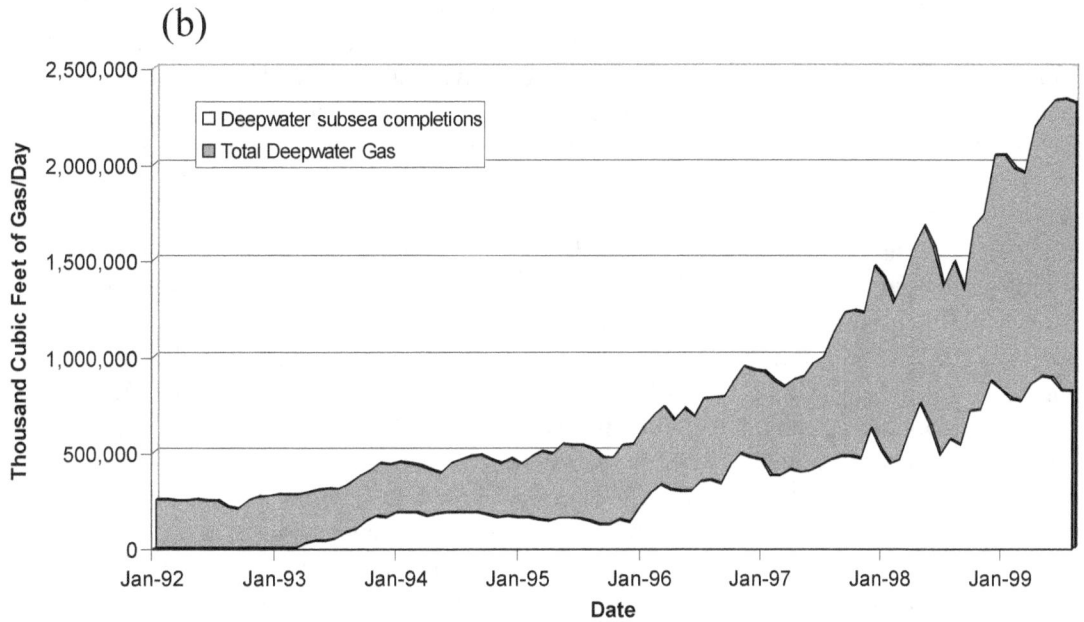

Figure 42. - Contributions from subsea completions toward total deepwater
(a) oil production and (b) gas production.

Deepwater oil and gas production was confined almost entirely to major oil and gas companies through 1996 (figures 43a and 43b). (Production volumes in figures 43a-b and 44a-b are attributed to companies on the basis of their percentage of lease ownership. For example, if Shell owned 75% of a particular lease in July 1997, then 75% of that lease's production was attributed to Shell that month.) In recent years, nonmajor companies significantly increased their deepwater oil production. Figures 44a and 44b show that nonmajor oil and gas companies contributed about 15 percent of deepwater oil production from 1992 through 1997. Nonmajor companies increased their share of deepwater oil production in 1998 and early 1999. On the contrary, nonmajor companies accounted for about 40 percent of deepwater gas production in early 1994. This percentage declined steadily until 1998 (primarily due to Shell's increased deepwater gas production). Nonmajor companies currently own about 25 percent of deepwater GOM oil production and about 20 percent of deepwater GOM gas production. Since there are significant lag times between leasing and production, and nonmajors did not gain a leasing foothold until about 1996 (figure 18), a surge of production from nonmajors could still be forthcoming.

Figures 45a and 45b display production contributions from each major oil and gas company. Shell and BP Amoco were the driving forces behind increasing deepwater production, with Shell as the clear leader in both oil and gas production. Shell's dominance in deepwater oil production began before 1992 and has continued throughout the 1990's. Shell's dominance in deepwater gas production began in the mid-1990's, and dramatically increased in 1997. Although BP Amoco's deepwater oil production started slightly behind Shell's, their oil production increases track one another throughout the 1990's (in part because Shell and BP Amoco have joint ownership in several large deepwater fields). Exxon Mobil currently runs a distant third in terms of deepwater GOM oil production, but is slightly ahead of BP Amoco in deepwater GOM gas production.

High well production rates have been a driving force behind the success of deepwater operations. Figure 46a illustrates the highest deepwater oil production rates each month since 1992. (Production rates in this report are daily averages from a full month of production.) For example, a well within Shell's Bullwinkle field produced about 5,000 barrels of oil per day (BOPD) in 1992. In 1994 a well within Shell's Auger field set a milestone, producing about 10,000 BOPD. Since 1994, maximum deepwater oil production rates continued to climb, especially in water depths between 1,500 and 4,999 ft. Note that there is currently no production in water depths greater than or equal to 7,500 ft and only minimal liquid production in water depths greater than or equal to 5,000 ft (from Shell's Mensa field, which primarily produces gas). Figure 46b shows similar production rates for gas. Maximum deepwater gas production rates hovered around 25 million cubic feet per day (MMCFPD) until a well in Shell's Popeye field bumped the deepwater production record to over 100 MMCFPD in 1996. Since then, the deeper waters yielded higher maximum production rates. In 1997, Shell's Mensa field showed the excellent potential for ultra-deepwater production rates. Note that the steep fluctuations in production rates within the 5,000-7,499 ft water depth category probably relate to the limited number of wells producing in this water depth range. That is, when

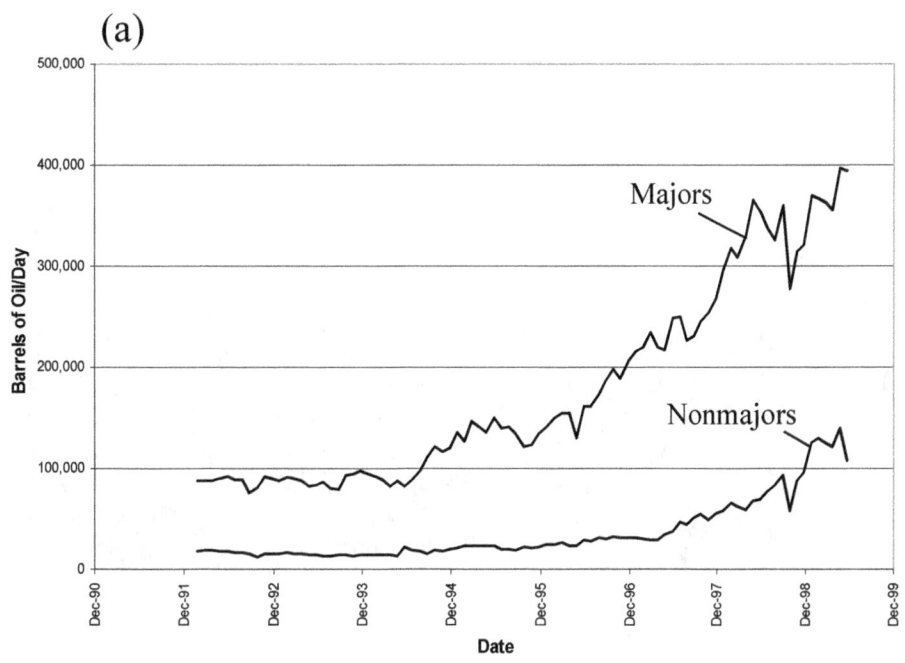

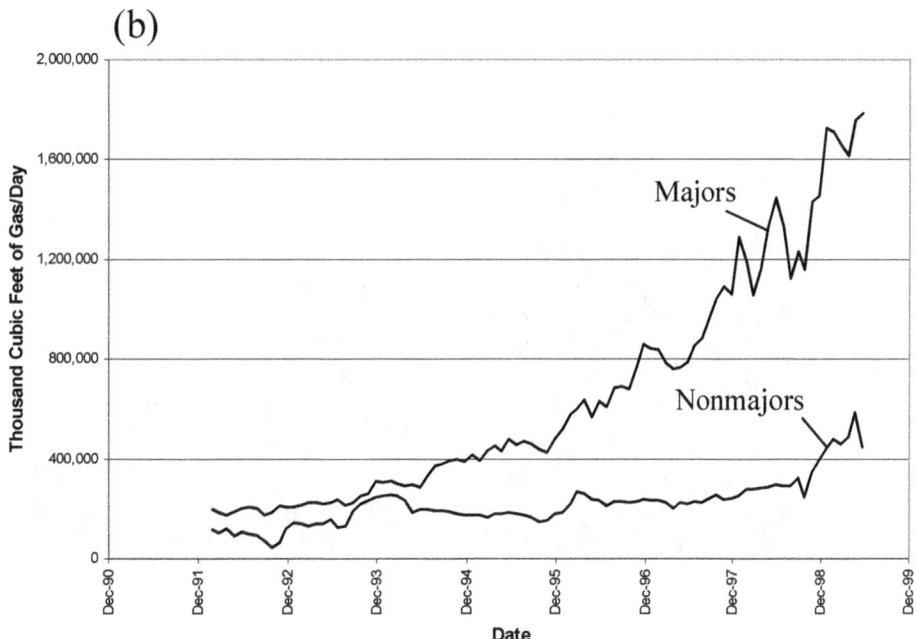

Figure 43. - Comparison of major companies and nonmajor companies in terms of deepwater (a) oil production and (b) gas production.

(a)

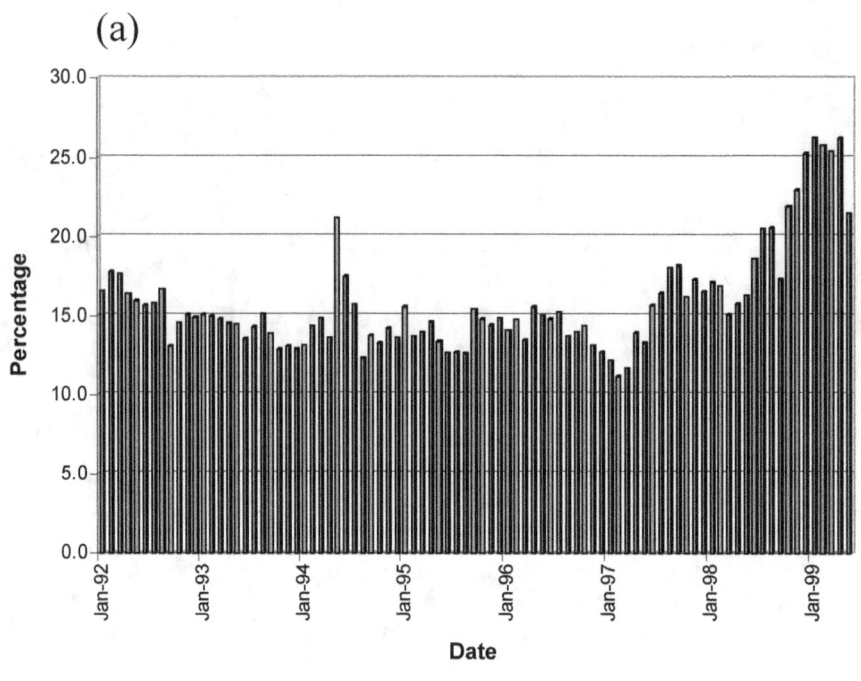

(b)

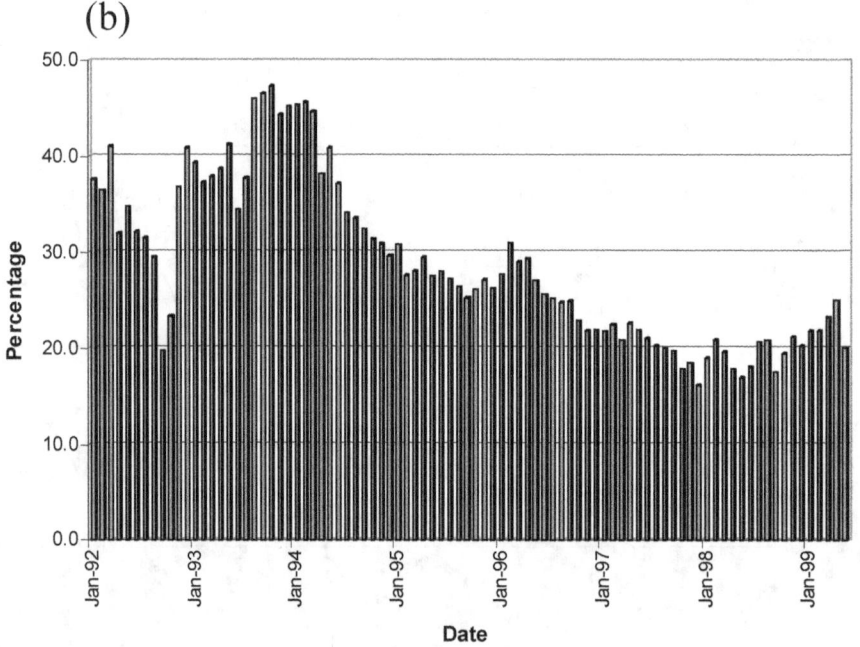

Figure 44. - Percentage of deepwater (a) oil production and (b) gas
production from nonmajor oil and gas companies.

58

(a)

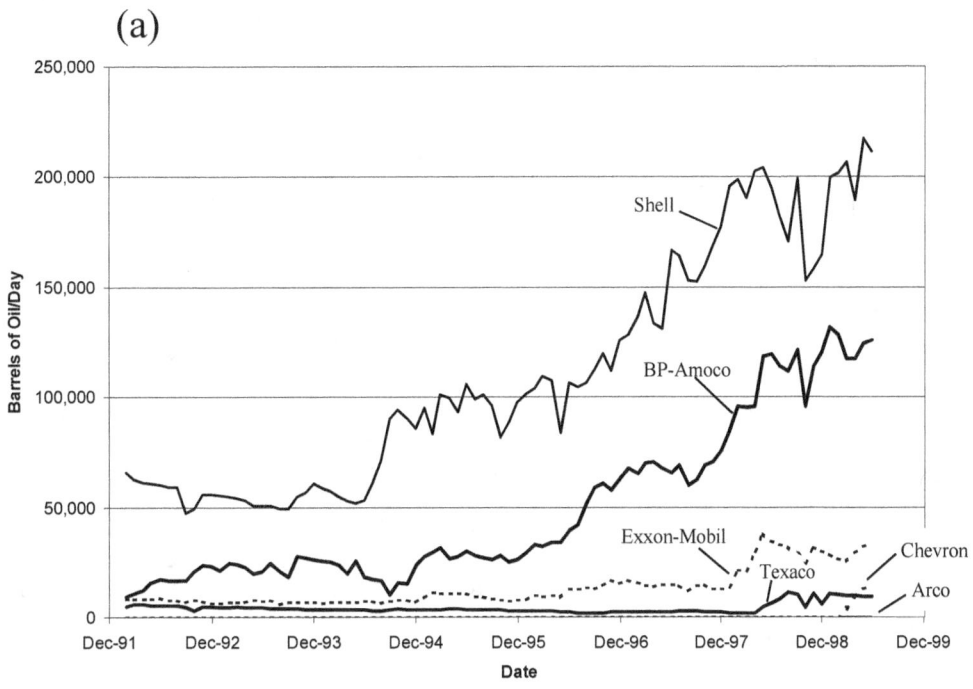

(b)

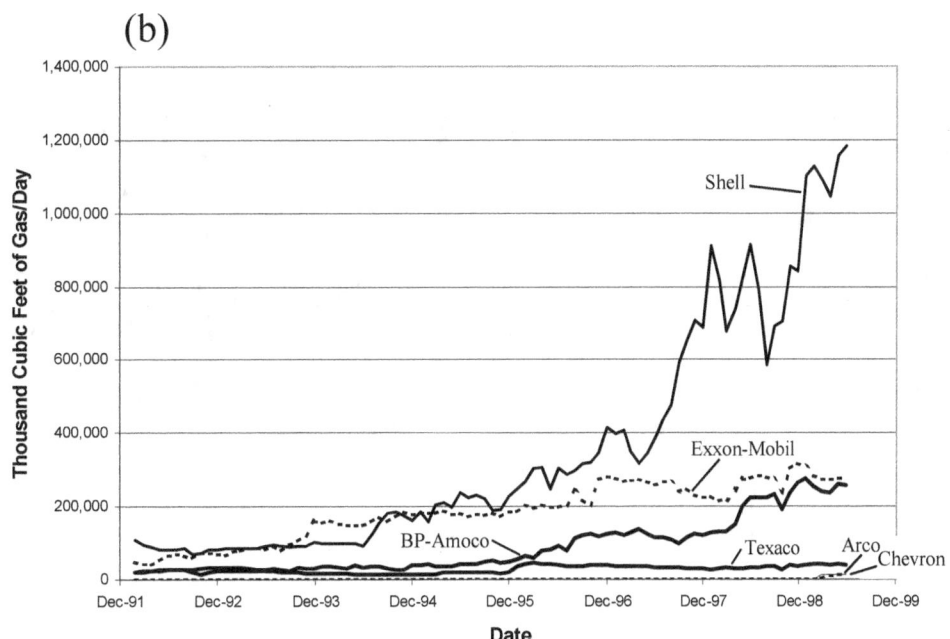

Figure 45. - Contributions from each major oil company toward total deepwater (a) oil production and (b) gas production.

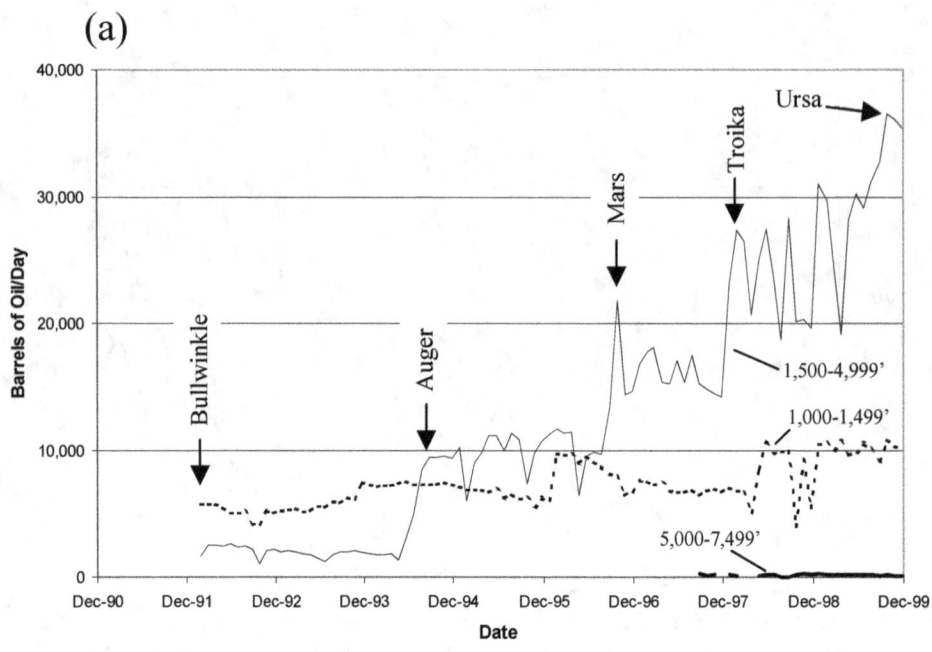

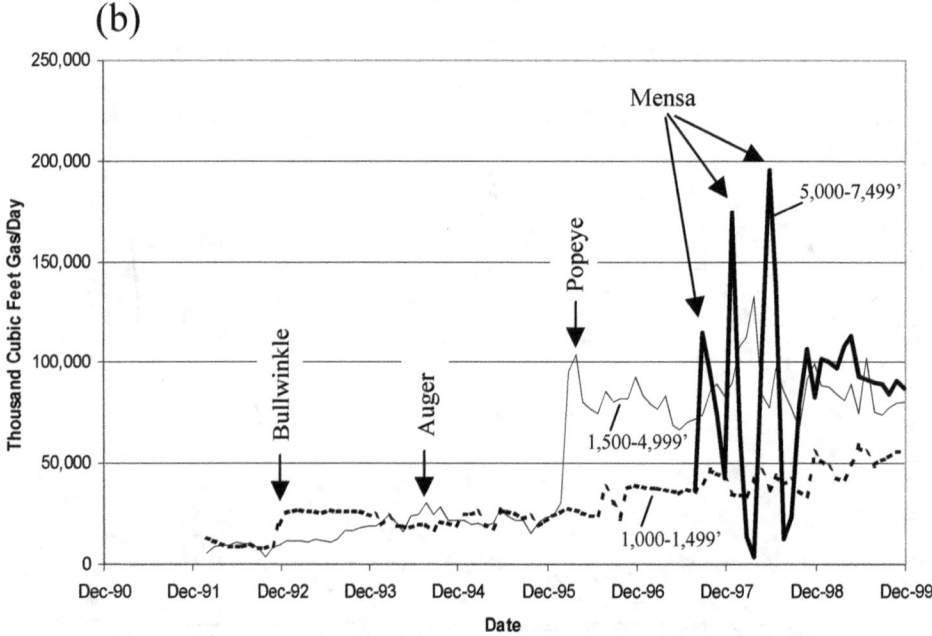

Figure 46. - Maximum production rates for a single well within each water depth category for deepwater (a) oil production and (b) gas production.

60

the only well on production is shut in for a short period of time, there are no other wells to become the maximum producer during the lull. Since the third Mensa well commenced production in late 1998, the maximum production rates in the 5,000-7,499 ft water depth range have stabilized at approximately 90 MMCFPD. To date, the daily oil production rate record for a single well is 36,520 BOPD (Ursa) and the record gas production rate is 196 MMCFPD (Mensa).

Figures 47 (oil) and 48 (gas) compare maximum historical production rates for each lease in the GOM. That is, the well with the highest historical production rate is shown for each lease. These maps show that many deepwater fields produce at higher rates than ever encountered in the GOM. Figure 47 also shows that maximum oil rates were significantly higher off the southeast Louisiana coast than off the Texas coast. This trend may change when Exxon's Hoover and Diana fields begin production. Figure 48 illustrates the high deepwater gas-production rates relative to the rest of the GOM. Note also the excellent production rates from the Norphlet trend (off the Alabama coast) and the Corsair trend (off the Texas coast).

Figures 49 (oil) and 50 (gas) depict the recent emergence of high deepwater production rates. Figure 49 shows the maximum oil production rates for all leases that produced over 5,000 BOPD. In 1996-1997 high oil production rates from deepwater wells began and immediately dominated the picture. Similarly, figure 50 shows the maximum gas production rates for all leases that produced over 75 MMCFPD. The significance of deepwater gas production rates began in 1996-1997 and continued through the present.

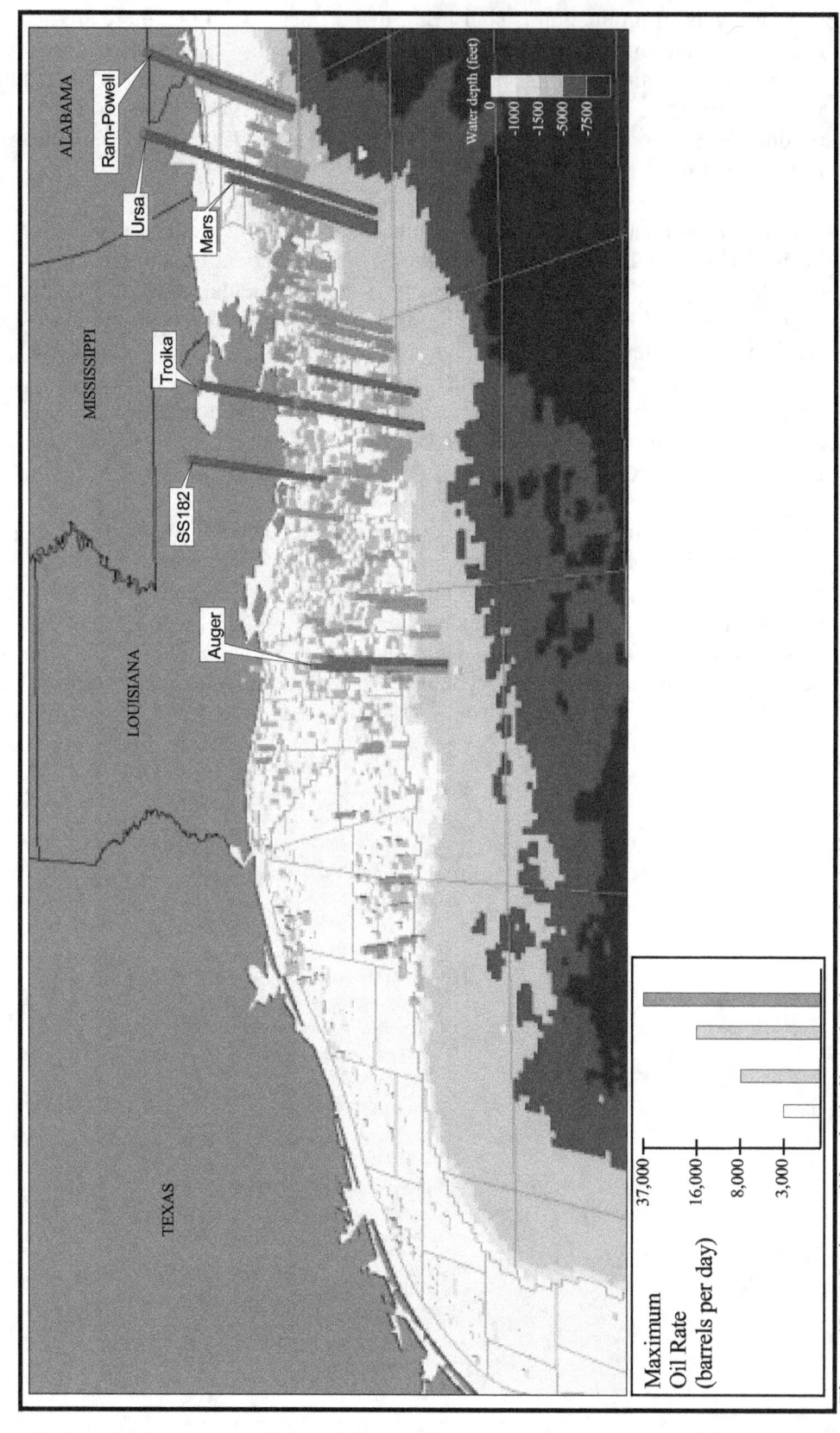

Figure 47. – Maximum historical oil production rates for Gulf of Mexico wells.

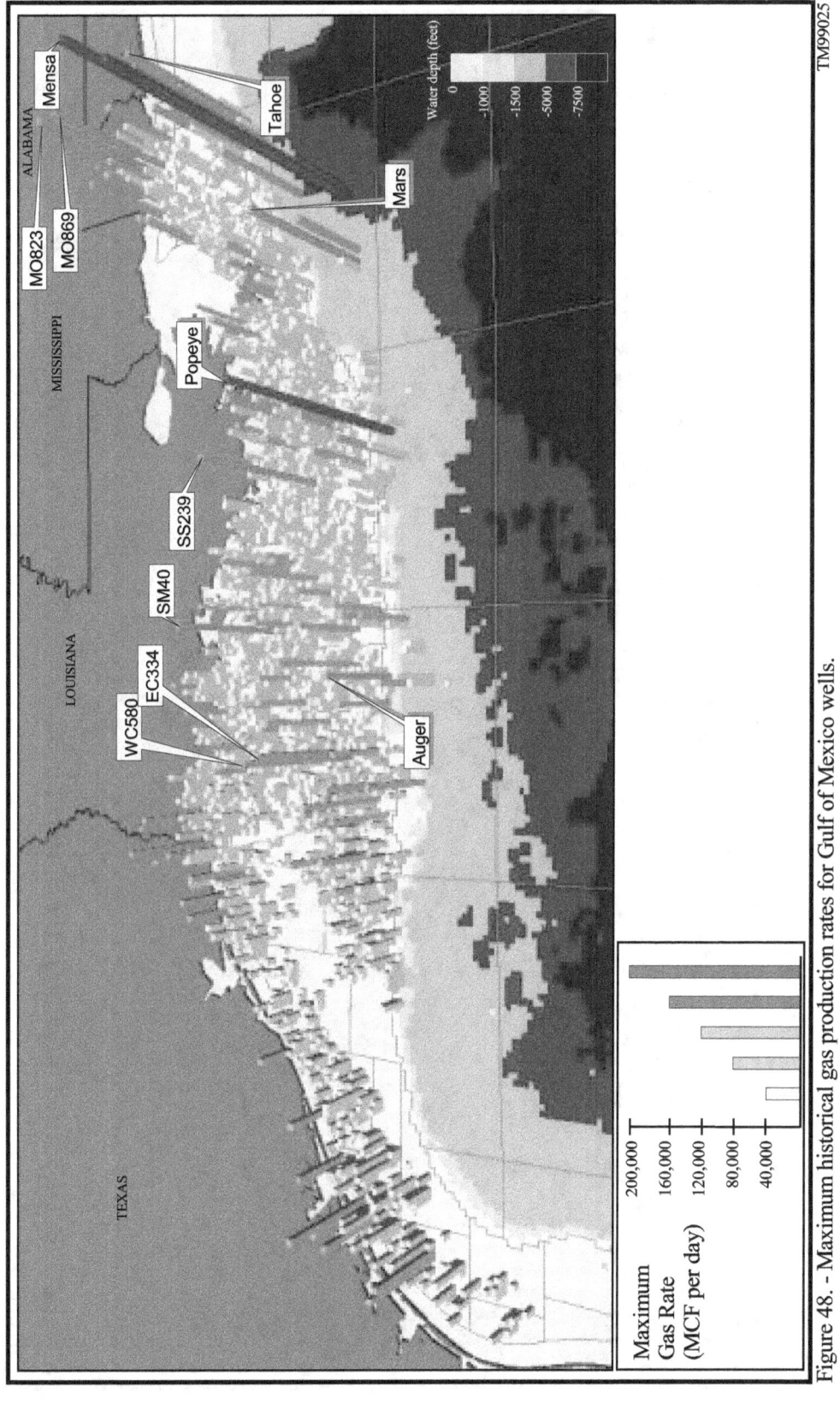

Figure 48. - Maximum historical gas production rates for Gulf of Mexico wells.

TM99025

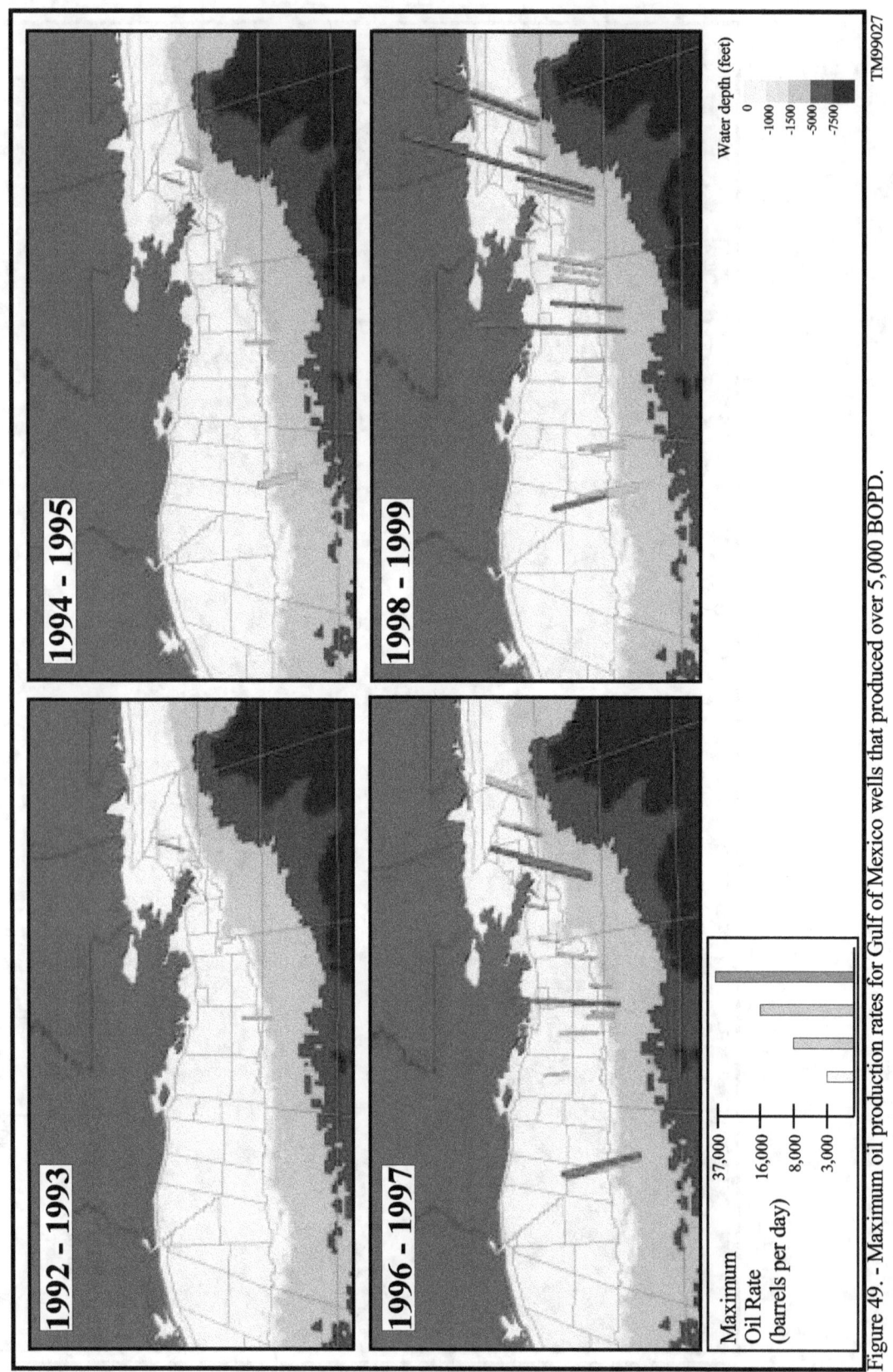

Figure 49. - Maximum oil production rates for Gulf of Mexico wells that produced over 5,000 BOPD.

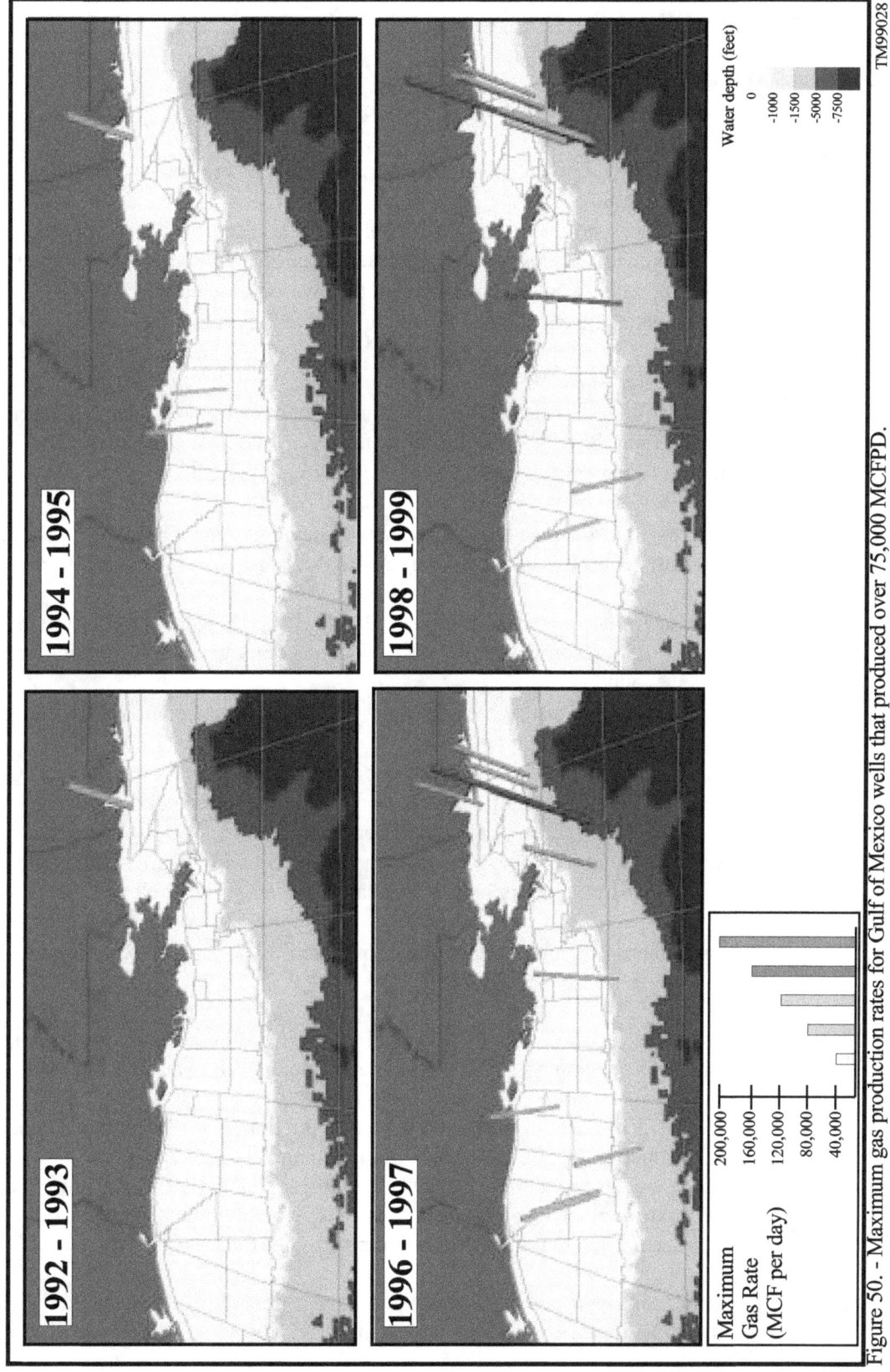

Figure 50. - Maximum gas production rates for Gulf of Mexico wells that produced over 75,000 MCFPD.

Summary and Conclusions

Thus far we discussed

- the emerging importance of the deepwater to overall Gulf of Mexico (GOM) oil and gas production,
- the historical trend in deepwater leasing toward increasing water depths and increased bid values,
- deepwater lease holdings of major oil and gas companies compared with nonmajor companies, showing the increased presence of nonmajor companies,
- the impact of recent company mergers on deepwater lease holdings,
- future deepwater lease availabilities and anticipated lease expirations,
- rapid increases in deepwater rig activity from 1992 through 1997, followed by modest increases since 1997,
- historical drilling statistics indicating significant increases in deepwater drilling activity and rapid leaps toward deeper waters,
- the increase in deepwater development activity, especially in regard to subsea completions,
- the progress of deepwater infrastructure development, especially pipelines reaching into deepwater in the Garden Banks Area and the entire Central Planning Area,
- the anticipated large deepwater reserve additions, especially when unproved reserves, known resources, and recent industry-announced discoveries are all taken into account,
- the large increase in average deepwater field sizes when compared with same-year shallow-water discoveries,
- the increasing contribution of deepwater oil and gas production toward total GOM production (Deepwater oil production recently surpassed shallow-water production for the first time in GOM history.),
- deepwater production from various companies, showing increasing production from majors and nonmajors, and historical domination by Shell and BP Amoco, and
- very high deepwater production rates compared with shallow-water production rates.

The remainder of this report combines historical leasing, drilling, development, reserve, and production data, revealing overall trends in deepwater activity and expectations.

Figure 51 illustrates deepwater projects that began production in 1999 and those expected to commence production soon (modified from Melancon and Baud, 2000). Nine deepwater projects began production in 1999, the largest single-year increase in history. Many more are expected in the next few years (several are not shown in figure 51 because operators requested that the information remain confidential).

Deepwater leasing activity accelerated in the late 1990's after Congress enacted the Deep Water Royalty Relief Act. The full effect of this leasing, however, will not be

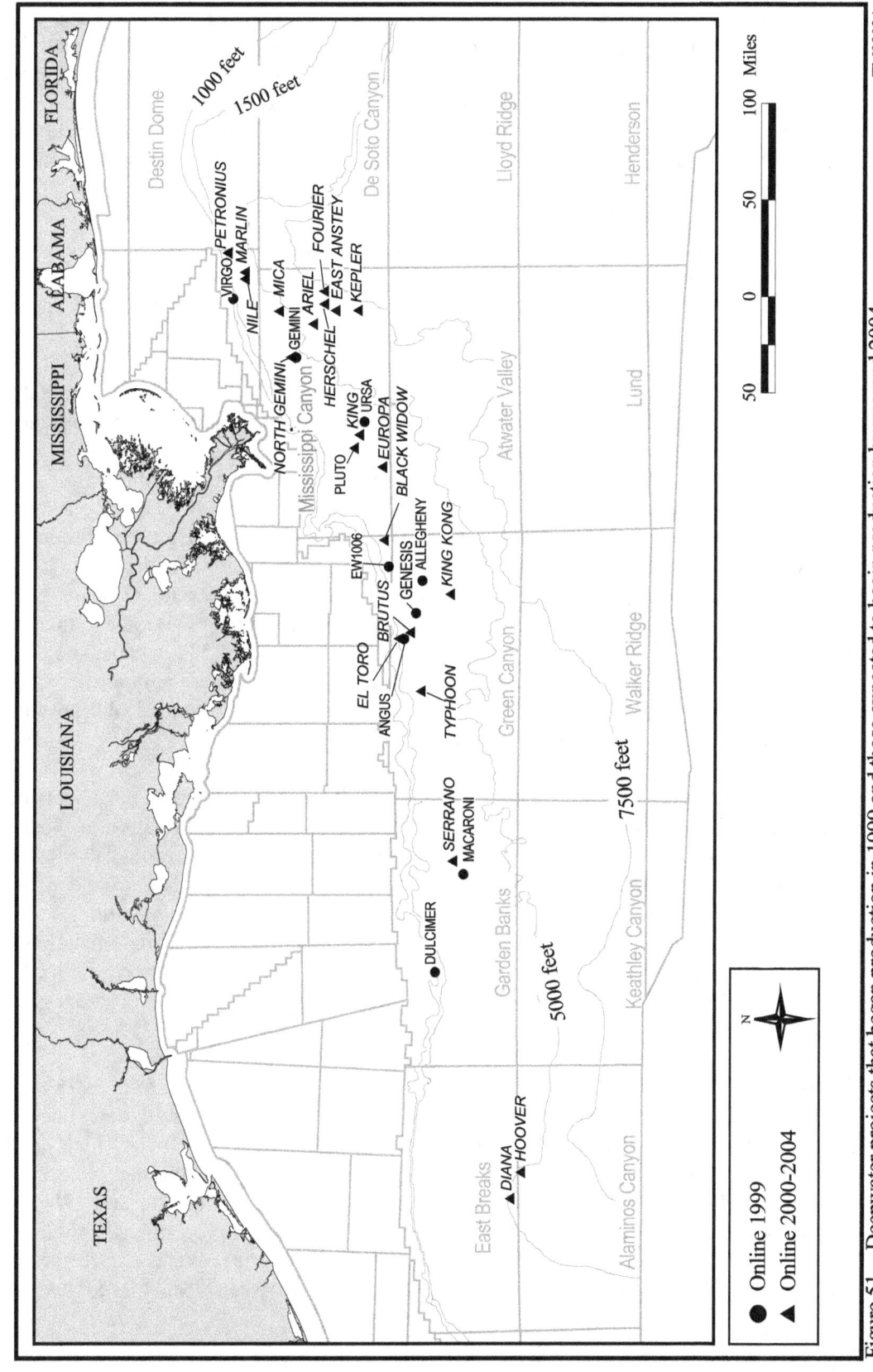

Figure 51. - Deepwater projects that began production in 1999 and those expected to begin production by yearend 2004.

67

realized for several years because there can be considerable lag times between leasing and first production, as illustrated in figure 52. There was considerable lease activity in the late 1980's. (Note that historic deepwater leasing shows no clear relation to average oil prices.) Acreage at Auger (Garden Banks 426 field) and Neptune (Atwater 575 field) were acquired in 1985 as part of this early activity. The first Auger well was drilled soon afterward, in 1987. Even though Auger was leased and drilled early, the first production didn't begin until 1994, about 10 years after the initial lease acquisition. The first Neptune well was not drilled until 1995, almost 10 years after the initial lease acquisition and no first production date has been made public. These time lags are not unusual with deepwater operations because of large lease inventories, the geologic and production uncertainties of frontier discoveries, the limited number of deepwater rigs, and the evolving deepwater development technology.

Figures 53a-c demonstrate average time lags associated with deepwater operations. These figures use data only from deepwater leases that have become productive. Figure 53a shows the average number of years it took to drill a well from the time the lease was issued. Figure 53b shows the average length of time from lease issue to qualification of the lease as productive (operators request that MMS qualify a lease as capable of production after drilling a discovery well and before beginning production). Figure 53c illustrates the time lags between leasing, qualification, and first production. Figure 53d uses a slightly different population; it plots the time lag for all leases drilled, all leases that qualified, and then leases that are productive. Obviously, there is a declining number of leases in each succeeding category in figure 53d because the number of leases drilled is higher than the number qualified, and the number of qualified leases is higher than the number of productive leases. The bar heights in figure 53d represent the total time elapsed since the leases were awarded.

There are two time lags represented in figures 53a-d. First, there is a lag between a deepwater discovery and the operator's request for lease qualification. Operators sometimes announce discoveries to the public long before qualifying the lease as productive with MMS (and thereby being granted field status). The second time lag depicted in figures 53a-d is the lag between leasing and subsequent operations (drilling, qualifying, and production). Note that, since deepwater leases are in effect for 8 or 10 years, the data are incomplete beyond about 1989. The apparent decreasing lag times for leases issued after 1989 are caused by the fact that the lease evaluation process is not yet complete.

The data show an increase in the number of years to drill the first well from 1976 to 1987 (figure 53a). This is probably a reflection of two factors. First, the earliest deepwater leases purchased were of very high interest to the lessees and, therefore, drilled quickly. Second, increasing lease inventories during the late 1980's meant that many leases could not be evaluated right away (increased deepwater leasing in the mid to late 1980's was probably related to the introduction of area-wide leasing procedures, the drop in minimum required bid from $150/acre to $25/acre, and the advent of 3-D seismic). Figure 53b shows similar trends in the time lags between lease issue and lease

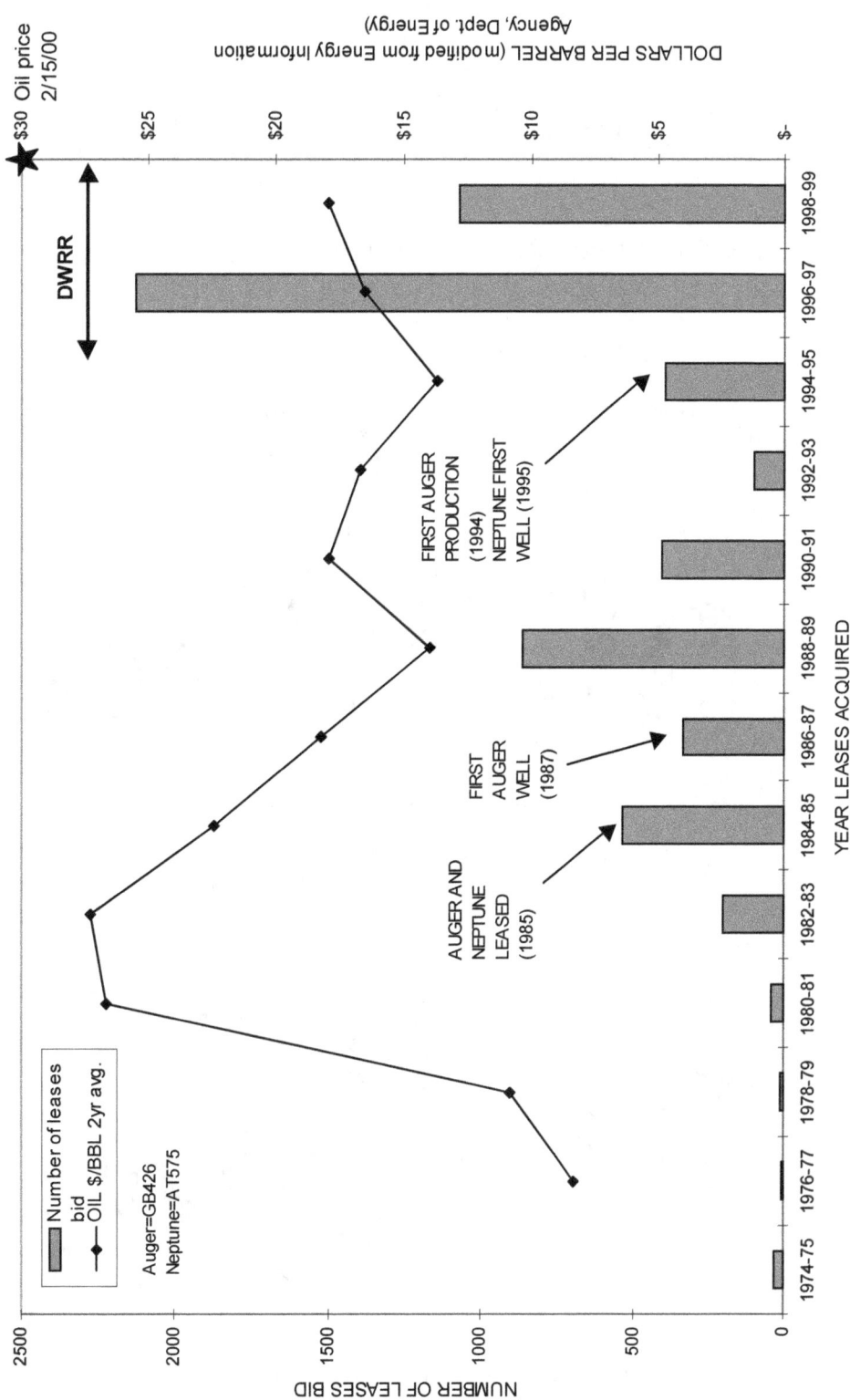

Figure 52. - Deepwater lease activity and oil prices.

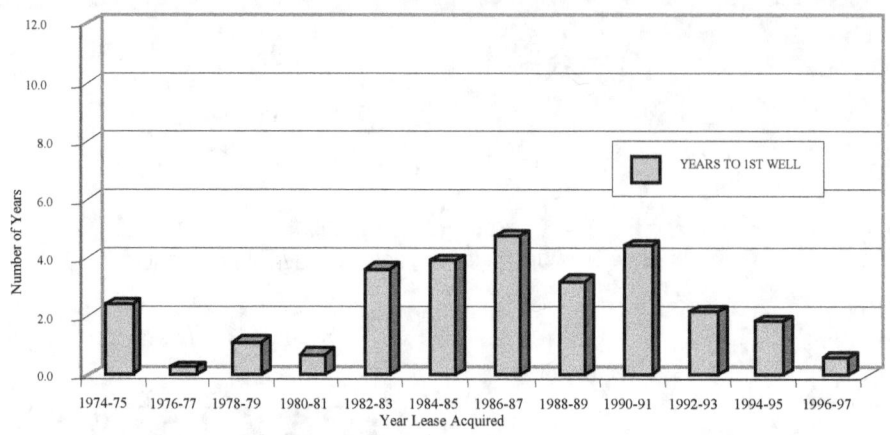

Figure 53a. - Time lag from leasing to first well
for producing deepwater fields.

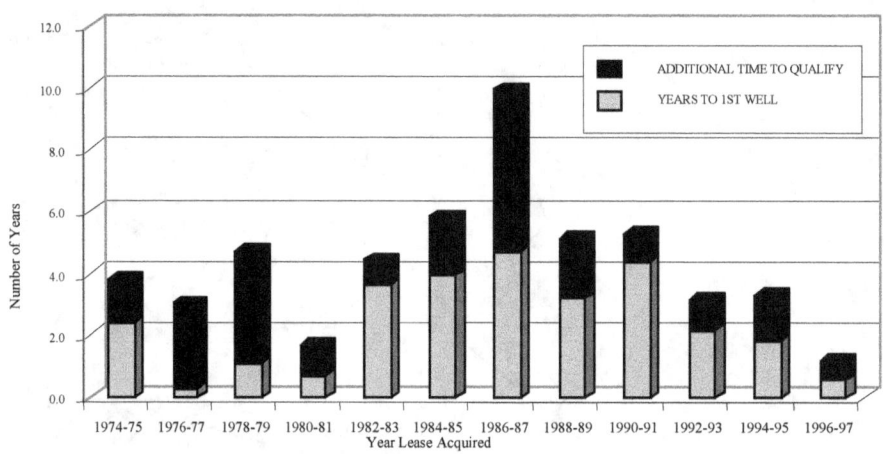

Figure 53b. - Time lag from leasing to qualifying for
producing deepwater fields.

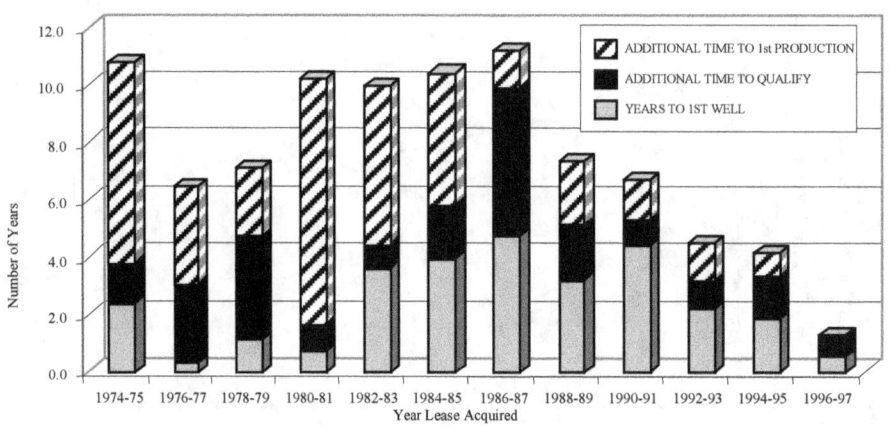

Figure 53c. - Time lag from leasing to first production for
producing deepwater fields.

70

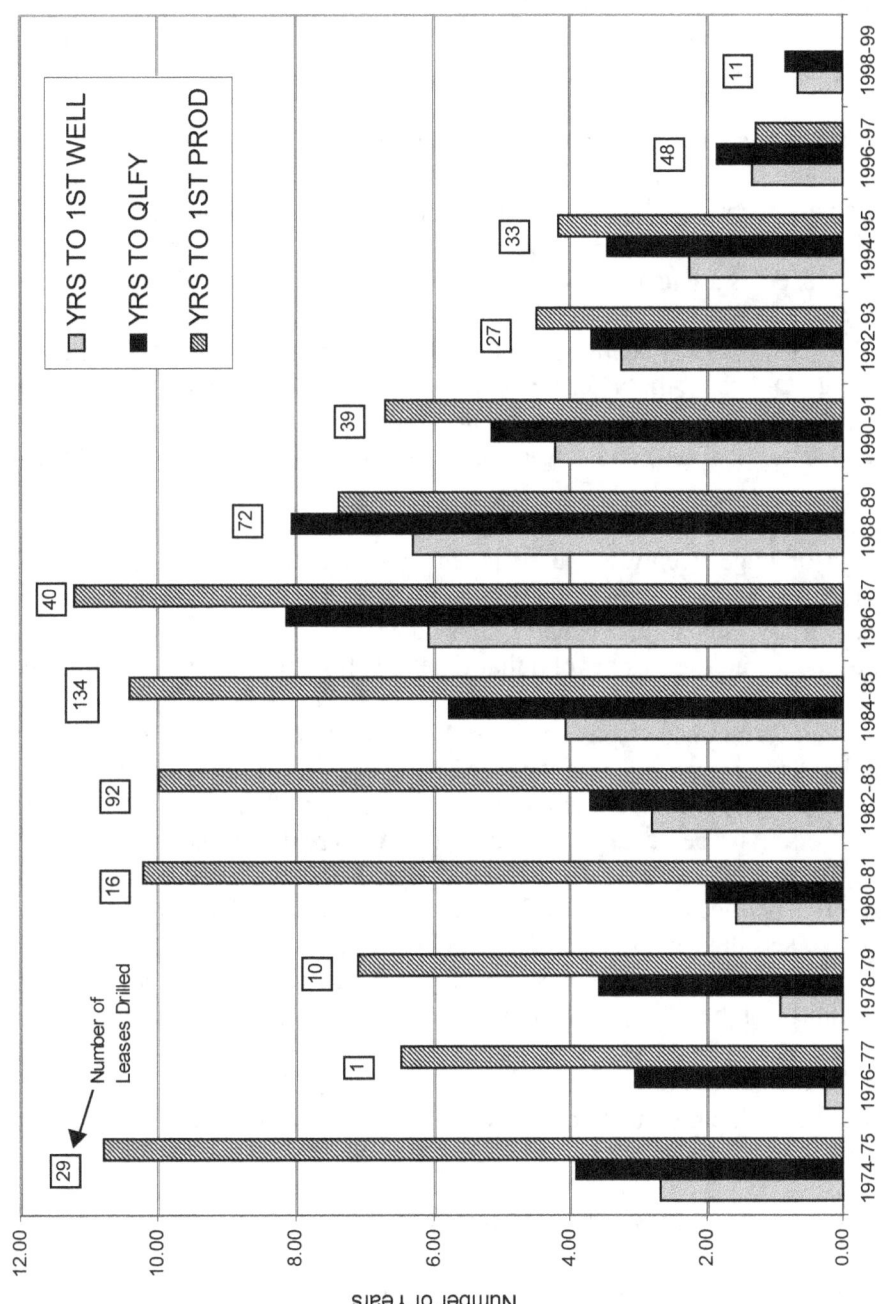

Figure 53d. - Time lag from leasing to first production, qualification and first production for all deepwater wells.

qualification. Exceptions include the long lag times between first drilling and qualifying from 1974 to 1979. During the 1980's there was also a gradual increase in the lag time between drilling of the first well and qualifying the lease. During most of the 1980's, it took about 10 to 11 years for the average field to come on production. It is important to note, however, that the time between drilling the first well and the beginning of production dropped significantly throughout the 1980's. That is, operators brought fields online in about 10 years, despite the fact that the first wells weren't drilled, on average, until about the fourth year of the lease term by the late 1980's.

Note that figure 53a indicates the first wells on leases that later produced were drilled about 4 years into the lease term during the late 1980's. However, figure 53d shows that the first wells on all deepwater leases (including those that never produced) were drilled about 6 years into the lease term during the late 1980's. This trend is expected, since the most promising prospects are usually drilled earlier in their lease terms.

In summary, the latest complete data indicate a 6-year average lag time between leasing and initial drilling. On leases that later become productive, the average lag time between leasing and initial drilling averages about 4 years. There is an additional 2-year average lag before the well is qualified, and a total of 10 to 11 years from lease issuance until production begins.

The combination of huge deepwater lease inventories and limited drilling capabilities means that numerous leases remain untested when their terms expire. Figure 54 shows historical lease activity trends. Once again, these data are complete only through about 1989, since most deepwater leases beyond that time are still under their primary term and still under evaluation. Over 90 percent of leases acquired in 1974-1975 and 1978-1979 were drilled. About 70 percent of leases acquired in 1974-1975 later qualified (indicating they discovered hydrocarbons) and about 50 percent came on production. Although less than 15 percent of the leases issued in 1976-1977 were ever drilled, they all qualified and came on production. The percentage of leases drilled decreased rapidly throughout the 1980's as lease inventories swelled. As the percentage of leases drilled decreased, so did the percentage of issued leases that qualified and the percentage that actually produced. By the late 1980's, less than 10 percent of issued deepwater leases were drilled, and less than 5 percent produced. This situation is probably caused by drilling limitations and the fact that only a finite number of leases can be evaluated within a given time frame.

Note that deepwater economics in the late 1980's was significantly different than it is today. Deepwater development technology was still in its infancy and the extraordinary deepwater production rates were yet to be realized.

Although the percentage of leases drilled decreased during the late 1980's, the actual number of leases drilled generally increased along with the number of leases issued. This eventually resulted in higher numbers of discoveries and producing leases from that crop of leases. These relationships are shown in figures 55a and 55b. Figure 55a shows that the number of leases issued through 1989 roughly correlated with the number of those leases that were eventually drilled. Similarly, Figure 55b indicates that the number of

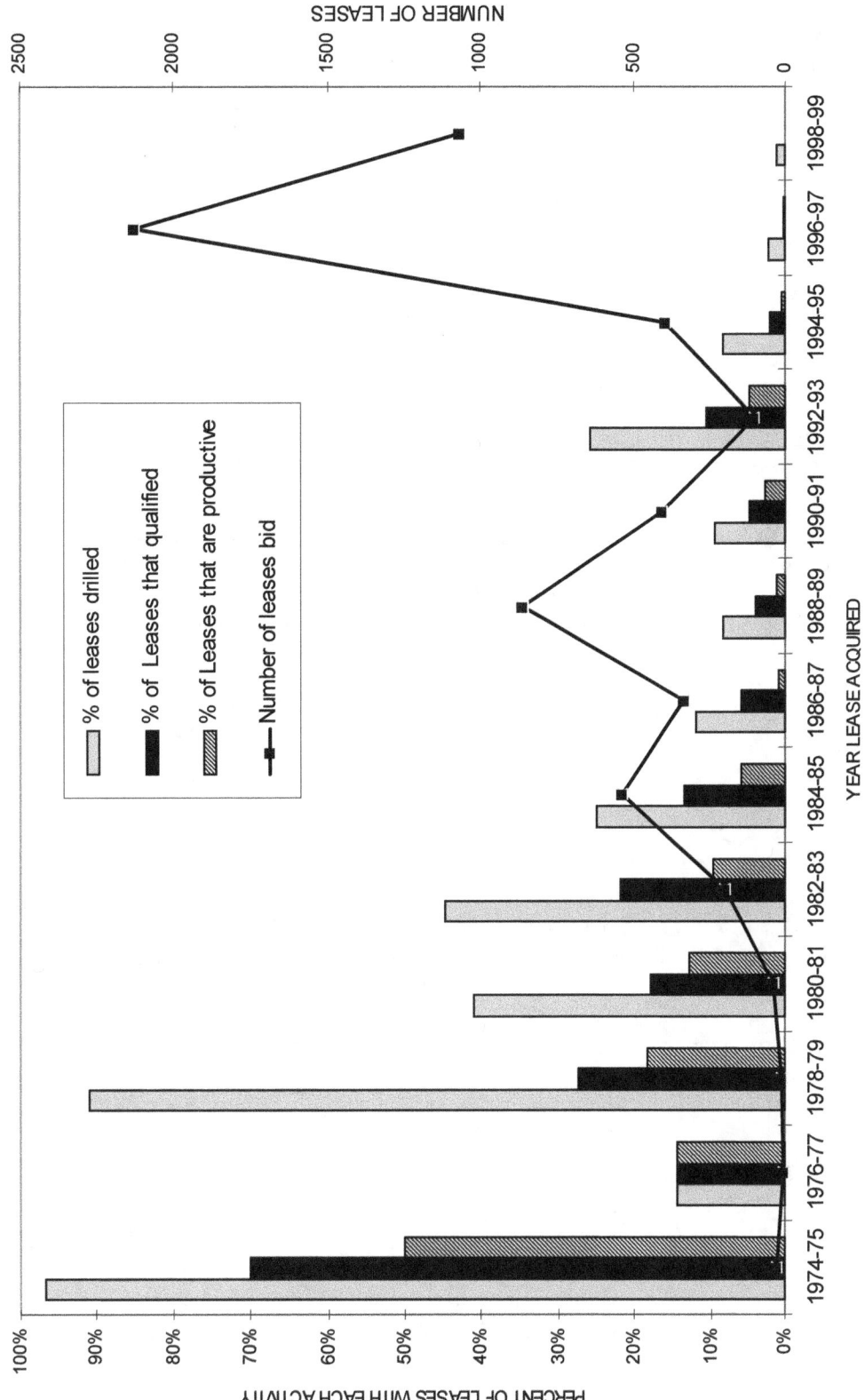

Figure 54. – Activity on deepwater leases.

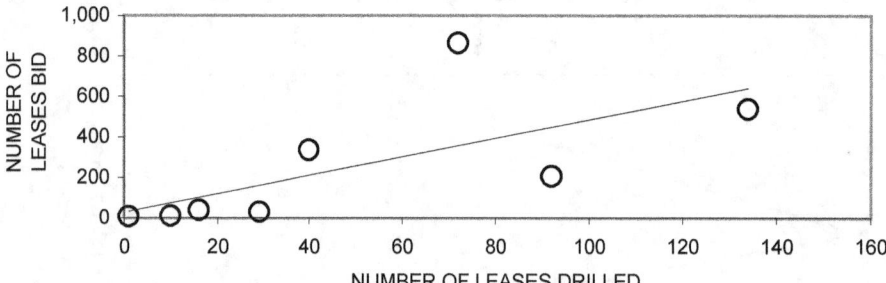

Figure 55a. - Relationship between number of leases bid upon (1974-1989) and number of leases drilled.

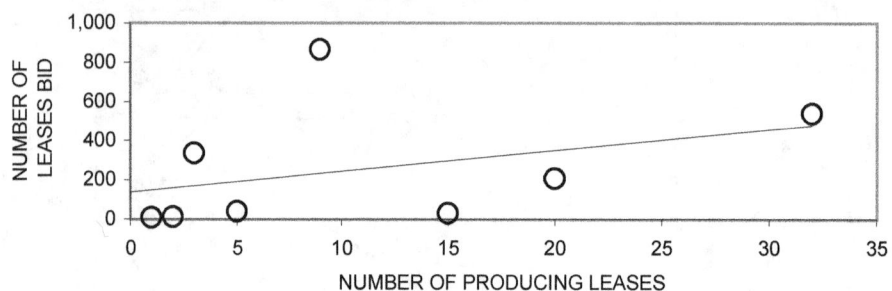

Figure 55b. - Relationship between number of leases bid upon and resulting number of producing leases.

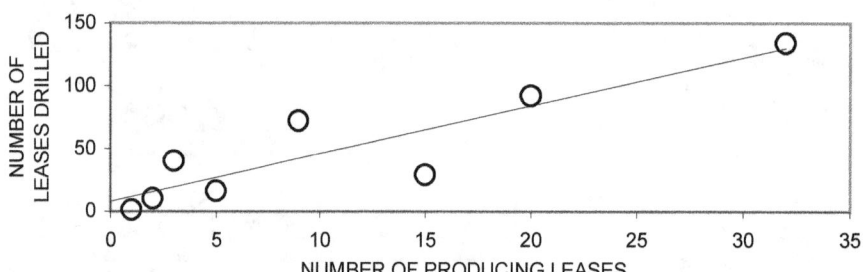

Figure 55c. - Relationship between number of leases drilled and resulting number of producing leases.

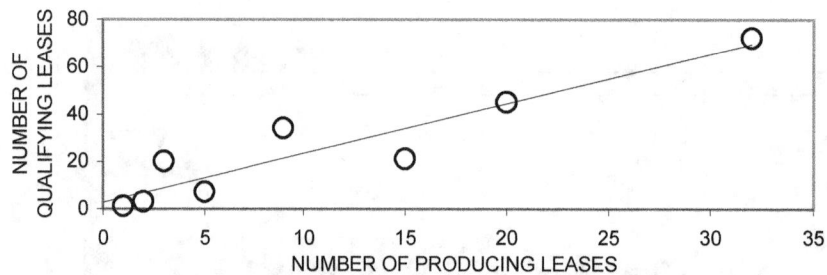

Figure 55d. - Relationship between number of qualifying leases and resulting number of producing leases.

leases issued through 1989 related to the number of those leases that eventually produced hydrocarbons.

As expected, the number of deepwater leases drilled from 1974 through 1989 correlated well with the number of those leases that later produced (figure 55c). Further, the number of leases that qualified as capable of production related very well with the number of those that eventually produced (figure 55d). In summary, historic data indicate that increased leasing leads directly to increased drilling, qualifying, and production (although not on a one-to-one basis).

Figure 56 shows the number of deepwater leases issued each year since 1992. This figure also projects the exploratory evaluation of these leases assuming that (a) each lease is drilled six years into its primary lease term (average from figure 53d), (b) 10 percent to 20 percent of these leases are eventually drilled (estimates from figure 54), and (c) future lease acquisitions will not significantly impact drilling of the existing lease inventory. Finally, we estimate the number of leases that can be evaluated by the anticipated GOM rig fleet. The highest number of deepwater exploratory wells drilled in one year was 109 wells on 75 different leases in 1998. During this year there were an average 28 deepwater rigs drilling at any given time. We anticipate a slight (11% over 1998 numbers) increase in the number of deepwater rigs drilling in the deepwater GOM through 2001. If we assume that new rigs will increase the number of exploratory wells drilled by 11 percent over record 1998 levels, then 83 deepwater leases could be evaluated each year.

On the basis of these assumptions, approximately 10 percent of the deepwater leases can be evaluated. This is consistent with the percentage of deepwater leases drilled in the late 1980's (the latest complete data). Since we assume all leases are drilled six years into their primary terms (the average from figure 53d), the apex of rig constraints is between 2002 and 2004. Operators may evaluate more than 10 percent of their deepwater lease inventory by spreading out their drilling programs wisely or bringing additional rigs into the GOM. In summary, deepwater rig availability is a limiting factor, but the percentage of leases that can be drilled with the expected GOM rig fleet is comparable to historic averages.

Despite the difficulty evaluating deepwater leases, the future of deepwater GOM exploration and production is very promising. Industry recently announced numerous deepwater discoveries. Field sizes and flow rates of deepwater discoveries are often outstanding. Although the traditional deepwater minibasin plays are far from mature, as several recent discoveries attest, new deepwater plays near and even beyond the Sigsbee Escarpment show that the deepwater GOM is still an emerging frontier. The Eastern Gulf lease sale in 2001 will open up additional deepwater acreage for the first competitive bidding in this area since 1988.

All phases of exploration and development moved steadily into deeper waters over the past eight years. This trend is evident in seismic activity, leasing, bid rejects, exploratory drilling, development drilling, discoveries, and production. Deepwater leasing was

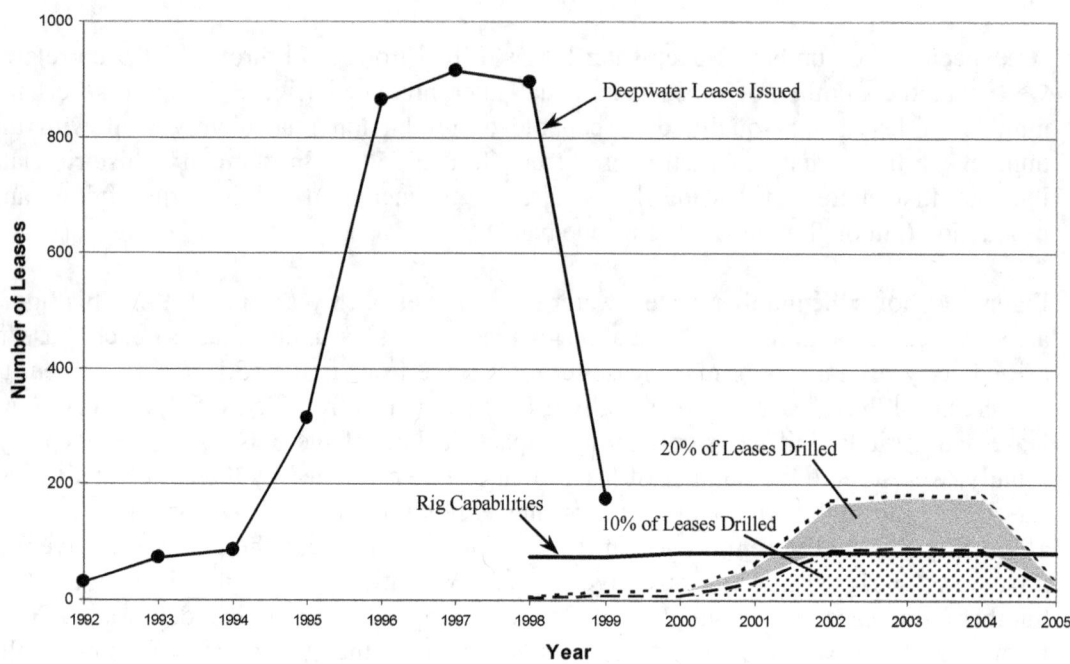

Figure 56. - Anticipated effect of rig constraints on lease evaluations.

almost exclusively the realm of major oil and gas companies until 1996, when nonmajors joined the trend. Major oil and gas companies continue to dominate deepwater production, but production from nonmajors should increase in a few years when anticipated discoveries on their 1996-1999 lease acquisitions begin producing.

The deepwater arena has come a long way in the past few years. The large volume of active deepwater leases, the steady drilling program, and the growing deepwater infrastructure all indicate that the deepwater GOM will continue to emerge as an integral part of this Nation's energy supply and remain one of the world's premier oil and gas basins.

Contributing Personnel

This report includes contributions from the following individuals.

Kim Altobelli
Alex Alvarado
Debbie Armond
Adrian Cottrill
Thierry DeCort
Scott Edwards
Holly Gaudet
Fred Jacobs
Eric Kazanis
Charles Leyendecker
Tara Montgomery
Michelle Morin
Mike Nixdorff
Paul Post
Jim Regg
Chris Schoennagel
Jim Swaney
Fred Times
Janice Todesco
Mike Tolbert
Warren Williamson
Chee Yu
Vicki Zatarian

References

Cranswick, D., and J. Regg, 1997, *Deepwater in the Gulf of Mexico: America's New Frontier*. Minerals Management Service, Gulf of Mexico OCS Region. OCS Report MMS 97-0004. New Orleans. 41 p.

Crawford, T. G., B. J. Bascle, C. J. Kinler, M. T. Prendergast, and K. M. Ross, 2000, *Estimated Oil and Gas Reserves, Gulf of Mexico, December 31, 1997*. Minerals Management Service, Gulf of Mexico OCS Region. OCS Report MMS 2000-006. New Orleans. 26 p.

Bollinger, D. B., 1999, "Demand for Marine Services Remains Volatile." *World Oil*. Vol. 220. No. 12. pp. 46-47.

DeLuca, M., 1999, "End of Mobile Drilling Unit Construction Cycle Nearing." *Offshore*. Vol. 59. No. 7. pp. 44-52.

Energy Information Agency, U.S. Department of Energy, "Domestic Crude Oil First Purchase Prices." Available: <<http://www.eia.doe.gov/pub/oil_gas/petroleum/data_publications/petroleum_marketing_monthly/current/txt/tables21.txt>>. February 2000.

Gulf of Mexico Weekly Rig Locator, 1999 (December), "Working Rigs and Locations by Rig Owner." Vol. 13. No. 49.

Harding, B. W., 1999, "Worldwide Mobile Fleet Capabilities Shifting Toward Deepwater." *Offshore*. Vol. 59. No. 7. pp. 54-76.

Hart's E&P Magazine, 1999 (December), "Gulf of Mexico Deep Production Sets Records." Vol. 72. No. 12. p. 17.

Kelly, P. L., 1999, "Big Challenges in the New Millennium." *World Oil*. Vol. 220. No. 12. pp. 39-40.

Melancon, J. M., and R. D. Baud, 2000, *Gulf of Mexico Outer Continental Shelf Daily Oil and Gas Production Rate Projections From 2000 Through 2004*. Minerals Management Service, Gulf of Mexico OCS Region. OCS Report MMS 2000-012. New Orleans. 20 p.

Minerals Management Service, 1999, "Gulf of Mexico Deep Water Oil and Gas Production Rises Dramatically." News Release. October 18, 1999. Office of Communications.

Rig Census, 1999 (December). Reed-Hycalog. Houston.

Appendix A – Announced Deepwater Discoveries and Fields

Nickname	Block	Operator	Water Depth	Field Discovery Date*	Year of First Production	Year of Last Production
Aconcagua	MC 305	Elf	7,039 ft			
Allegheny	GC 254	British-Borneo	3,186 ft	Jan-85	1999	
AmberJack	MC 109	BP Exploration	1,058 ft	Jul-84	1991	
Angus	GC 112	Shell Deepwater Dev. Inc.	1,465 ft	Jun-97	1999	
Ariel/Nakika	MC 429	Shell Deepwater Dev. Inc.	6,274 ft	Nov-95		
Arnold	EW 963	Marathon	1,752 ft	Jun-96	1998	
Atlantis	GC 699	BP-Amoco	6,133 ft			
Auger	GB 426	Shell Deepwater Prod. Inc.	2,864 ft	May-87	1994	
Baha	AC 600	Shell	7,620 ft	May-96		
Baldpate	GB 260	Amerada Hess	1,605 ft	Nov-91	1998	
Bison	GC 166	BP-Amoco	2,518 ft	Mar-86		
Black Widow	AT 1	Mariner	1,850 ft	May-86	2000	
Boomvang	EB 688	Kerr-McGee	3,665 ft	May-88		
Brutus	GC 158	Shell Deepwater Prod. Inc.	2,877 ft	Mar-89	2001	
Bullwinkle	GC 65	Shell Offshore Inc.	1,330 ft	Oct-83	1989	
Camden Hills	MC 348	Marathon	7,200 ft			
Cognac	MC 194	Shell Offshore Inc.	1,023 ft	Jul-75	1979	
Cooper	GB 387	EEX	2,163 ft	Mar-89	1995	1999
Coulomb	MC 657	Shell	7,500 ft	Nov-87		
Crazy Horse	MC 778	BP-Amoco	6,044 ft			
Crosby	MC 899	BP-Amoco	4,165 ft	Jan-98		
Diamond	MC 445	Oryx	2,095 ft	Dec-92	1993	1999
Diana	EB 945	Exxon	4,679 ft	Aug-90		
Dulcimer	GB 367	Mariner	1,124 ft	Feb-98	1999	
East Anstey/Nakika	MC 607	Shell Deepwater Dev. Inc.	6,590 ft	Nov-97		
El Toro	GC 69	Shell Deepwater Dev. Inc.	1,428 ft	Sep-84		
Europa	MC 935	Shell Deepwater Prod. Inc.	3,883 ft	Apr-94	2000	
Fourier/Nakika	MC 522	Shell Deepwater Dev. Inc.	6,950 ft	Jul-89		
Fuji	GC 506	Texaco	4,243 ft	Jan-95		
Gemini	MC 292	Texaco	3,745 ft	Sep-95	1999	
Genesis	GC 205	Chevron	2,599 ft	Sep-88	1999	
Glider	GC 248	Shell	3,300 ft			
Gomez	MC 755	Union Pacific	3,010 ft	Mar-86		
Grand Canyon	GC 141	Conoco	1,715 ft			
Habanero	GB 341	Shell	2,000 ft			
Herschel/Nakika	MC 520	Shell Deepwater Dev. Inc.	6,739 ft			
Holstein	GC 644	BP-Amoco	4,292 ft	Feb-99		
Hoover	AC 25	Exxon	4,795 ft	Jan-97		
Horn Mountain	MC 127	Vastar	5,443 ft			
Jolliet	GC 184	Conoco	1,722 ft	Jul-81	1989	
K2	GC 562	Conoco	3,979 ft			
Kepler/Nakika	MC 383	Shell Deepwater Dev. Inc.	5,759 ft	Aug-87		
King	MC 084	Amoco Production	5,315 ft	Jan-93		
King	MC 764	Shell Deepwater Dev. Inc.	3,265 ft		2000	
King Kong	GC 472	Shell Deepwater Dev. Inc.	3,817 ft	Feb-89		
King's Peak	DC 133	Amoco Production	6,608 ft	Mar-93		
Knight	GB 372	Santa Fe	1,740 ft			
Lena	MC 281	Exxon	1,017 ft	May-76	1984	
Leo	MC 546	British Borneo	2,496 ft	Feb-86		
Macaroni	GB 602	Shell Deepwater Dev. Inc.	3,600 ft		1999	
Mad Dog	GC 826	BP-Amoco	6,560 ft	Nov-98		
Madison	AC 24	Exxon	4,851 ft	Jun-98		
Magnolia	GB 783	Conoco	4,668 ft	May-99		
Marlin	VK 915	Amoco Production	3,238 ft	Jun-93	2000	
Mars	MC 807	Shell Deepwater Prod. Inc.	2,958 ft	Apr-89	1996	
Marshall	EB 949	Exxon	4,376 ft	Jul-98		
Matterhorn	MC 243	Elf	3,100 ft	Sep-90		
McKinley	GC 416	Union	4,019 ft	Aug-98		
Medusa	MC 582	Murphy	2,100 ft			

Mensa	MC 731	Shell Deepwater Prod. Inc.	5,330 ft	Dec-86	1997	
Metallica	MC 911	BP-Amoco	7,000 ft			
Mica	MC 167	Exxon	4,356 ft			
Mickey	MC 211	Exxon	4,356 ft	May-90		
Mirage	MC 941	Vastar	3,914 ft			
Morpeth/Klamath	EW 921	British-Borneo	1,706 ft	Feb-91	1998	
Nansen	EB 602	Kerr-McGee	3,680 ft			
Neptune	AT 575	BP-Amoco	6,220 ft	Sep-95		
Neptune/Thor	VK 825	Kerr-McGee	1,866 ft	Nov-87	1997	
Nile	VK 914	BP-Amoco	3,534 ft	Apr-97	2001	
Nirvana	MC 162	BP-Amoco	3,517 ft	Nov-94		
North Gemini	MC 248	Chevron	3,290 ft		2001	
Northwestern	GB 200	Amerada Hess	1,471 ft	May-98		
Oregano	GB 559	Shell	3,400 ft			
Petronius	VK 786	Texaco	1,754 ft	Jul-95		
Pluto/Blood Sweat & Tears	MC 718	Mariner	2,786 ft	Oct-95	2000	
Pompano/Pompano II	VK 990	BP Exploration	1,445 ft	May-81	1994	
Popeye	GC 116	Shell Deepwater Prod. Inc.	2,067 ft	Feb-85	1996	
Poseidon	GC 691	BP-Amoco	4,489 ft	Feb-96		
Ram Powell	VK 956	Shell Deepwater Prod. Inc.	3,247 ft	May-85	1997	
Rocky	GC 110	Shell Deepwater Prod. Inc.	1,621 ft	Aug-87	1996	
Salsa/Congor	GB 171	Kerr-McGee	1,074 ft	Apr-84	1998	
Seattle Slew	EW 914	Tatham	1,019 ft	Aug-84	1993	1997
Serrano	GB 516	Shell Deepwater Dev. Inc.	3,153 ft	Jul-96		
Sunday Silence	EW 958	Sonat	1,464 ft	Jul-94		
Tahoe/Tahoe II	VK 783	Shell Deepwater Prod. Inc.	1,492 ft	Dec-84	1994	
Troika	GC 244	BP Exploration	2,681 ft	May-94	1997	
Typhoon	GC 236	Chevron	2,005 ft	May-98	2001	
Ursa	MC 810	Shell Deepwater Prod. Inc.	3,885 ft	Oct-90	1999	
Virgo	VK 823	Elf	1,154 ft	May-97	1999	
Zinc	MC 354	Exxon	1,478 ft	Aug-77	1993	
	AT 008	Shell	3,135 ft	Apr-97		
	EB 377	Shell	2,450 ft	Oct-85		
	EB 992	Exxon	4,872 ft	Nov-95		
	EW 1006	Walter Oil & Gas	1,832 ft	Jan-88	1999	
	GB 208	Agip	1,270 ft	Sep-91		
	GB 254	Chevron	1,920 ft	Jul-93		
	GB 269	Texaco	1,036 ft	Mar-96		
	GB 302	Conoco	2,411 ft	Feb-91		
	GB 379	Conoco	2,076 ft	Jul-85		
	GB 409	Texaco	1,357 ft	May-97		
	GB 412	Union	1,313 ft	Jul-84		
	GB 543	Conoco	2,000 ft			
	GC 021	Odeco	1,193 ft	Oct-84		
	GC 027	Agip	1,593 ft	Jul-89		
	GC 029	Placid	1,554 ft	Jan-84	1988	1990
	GC 037	British Borneo	2,024 ft			
	GC 039	Placid	1,917 ft	Apr-84		
	GC 070	Conoco	1,874 ft	Jun-84		
	GC 075	Oryx	2,172 ft	May-85	1988	1989
	GC 082	British Borneo	2,400 ft			
	GC 147	Texaco	1,275 ft	May-88		
	GC 153	Marathon	1,500 ft			
	GC 153	Marathon	1,609 ft	Apr-84		
	GC 162	Maxus (US)	2,578 ft	Jul-89		
	GC 228	Texaco	1,638 ft	Jul-85		
	GC 235	Placid	1,690 ft	Oct-84		
	GC 463	BP-Amoco	4,032 ft	Dec-98		
	MC 026	BP-Amoco	1,272 ft	May-94		
	MC 113	Placid	1,857 ft	Jan-76		
	MC 285	Texaco	3,068 ft	Sep-87		
	MC 442	EEX	1,531 ft			
	MC 455	Union	1,400 ft	Feb-86		
	MC 709	Arco	2,544 ft	Feb-87		
	MC 929	Conoco	2,250 ft	Nov-87		

	MC 942	Shell	3,930 ft			
	PI 525	BP-Amoco	3,430 ft	Apr-96		
	VK 742	Texaco	1,004 ft	Aug-97		
	VK 862	Walter Oil & Gas	1,043 ft	Oct-76	1995	
	VK 864	Conoco	1,482 ft	Oct-81		
	VK 873	Shell	3,810 ft	Mar-88		

* The absence of a field discovery date indicates an industry-announced discovery without a qualified well on the lease. These discoveries have not necessarily been confirmed by MMS and they are not yet classified as fields by MMS.

Appendix B – Companies Defined as Majors in this Report

Group Name	Company Name	MMS Number
Arco	ARCO Pipe Line Company	00486
Arco	Atlantic Richfield Company	00002
Arco	Atlantic Richfield Company	00967
Arco	The Atlantic Refining Company	00002
Arco	Vastar Offshore, Inc.	02316
Arco	Vastar Pipeline, LLC	02317
Arco	Vastar Resources, Inc.	01855
BP Amoco	Amoco Canyon Company	00735
BP Amoco	Amoco Corporation	02244
BP Amoco	Amoco Foundation, Inc.	01679
BP Amoco	Amoco Pipeline Company	00751
BP Amoco	Amoco Production Company	00114
BP Amoco	BP Alaska Exploration Inc.	00301
BP Amoco	BP Amoco Corporation	02367
BP Amoco	BP Exploration & Oil Inc.	01680
BP Amoco	BP Exploration Inc.	00593
BP Amoco	BP Exploration U.S.A., Inc.	00120
BP Amoco	BP Oil Company	01680
BP Amoco	BP Oil Corporation	00120
BP Amoco	BP Prod. Corp.	02350
BP Amoco	Sohio Alaska Petroleum Company	00113
BP Amoco	Sohio Natural Resources	00113
BP Amoco	Sohio Petroleum Company	00113
BP Amoco	Sohio Petroleum Company	00593
Chevron	Chevron Corporation	02335
Chevron	Chevron Oil Company	00078
Chevron	Chevron Oil Company of the Netherlands	01443
Chevron	Chevron PBC, Inc.	01750
Chevron	Chevron Pipe Line Company	00400
Chevron	Chevron U.S.A. Inc.	00078
Chevron	Gulf Oil Corporation	00112
Exxon Mobil	Exxon Asset Holdings LLC	02356
Exxon Mobil	Exxon Asset Management Company	02295
Exxon Mobil	Exxon Corporation	00276
Exxon Mobil	Exxon Pipeline Company	00103
Exxon Mobil	Mobil Corporation	02221
Exxon Mobil	Mobil E&P U.S. Development Corporation	02203
Exxon Mobil	Mobil E&P U.S. Development Fund, L.P.	02209
Exxon Mobil	Mobil Eugene Island Pipeline Company	00883
Exxon Mobil	Mobil Exploration And Producing North America Inc.	01055
Exxon Mobil	Mobil Foundation, Inc.	01933
Exxon Mobil	Mobil-GC Corporation	00565
Exxon Mobil	Mobil NOC Inc.	00021
Exxon Mobil	Mobil Oil Corporation	00039
Exxon Mobil	Mobil Oil Exploration & Producing Southeast Inc.	00540
Exxon Mobil	Mobil Producing Texas & New Mexico Inc.	00565
Exxon Mobil	Mobil-TransOcean Company	00637
Exxon Mobil	Superior Oil Company	00047

Shell	Shell Consolidated Energy Resources Inc.	01940
Shell	Shell Deepwater Development Inc.	02139
Shell	Shell Deepwater Production Inc.	02140
Shell	Shell Energy Resources Inc.	00688
Shell	Shell Frontier Oil & Gas Inc.	01728
Shell	Shell Gas Gathering Company	02168
Shell	Shell Gas Pipeline Company	01070
Shell	Shell Land & Energy Company	01967
Shell	Shell Offshore Inc.	00689
Shell	Shell Offshore Properties and Capital II, Inc.	02128
Shell	Shell Oil Company	00117
Shell	Shell Pipe Line Corporation	00124
Shell	Shell Seahorse Company	02147
Shell	Shell Western E&P Inc.	00832
Texaco	Four Star Oil & Gas Company	00005
Texaco	Four Star Oil & Gas Company	00005
Texaco	Getty Oil Company	00005
Texaco	Getty Pipeline, Inc.	01107
Texaco	Getty Reserve Oil, Inc.	00578
Texaco	Texaco Inc.	00040
Texaco	Texaco Oils Inc.	00857
Texaco	Texaco Pipeline Inc.	01107
Texaco	Texaco Producing Inc.	00771
Texaco	Texaco Seaboard Inc.	00025
Texaco	Texaco Trading and Transportation, Inc.	02020

Appendix C – Subsea Completions

Area	Block	Well Name	API Number	Operator	Completion Date	Water Depth
BA	806	004	427024024500	Vastar Resources, Inc.	1997	164 ft
EB	112	003	608044015700	Agip Petroleum Co. Inc.	1996	638 ft
EB	117	001	608044016102	Vastar Offshore, Inc.	1997	570 ft
EB	157	002	608044015200	Agip Petroleum Co. Inc.	1996	941 ft
EB	168	001	608044016600	Walter Oil & Gas Corporation	1997	450 ft
EB	A 124	001	427124010700	Walter Oil & Gas Corporation	1993	381 ft
EC	235	001	177034047300	Chevron U.S.A. Inc.	1986	121 ft
EC	328	005	177044080800	Louis Dreyfus Natural Gas Corp.	1997	243 ft
EC	341	001	177044067100	Walter Oil & Gas Corporation	1988	275 ft
EC	388	A002	608074015601	EEX Corporation	1997	2,096 ft
EI	175	004	177090084200	Vastar Resources, Inc.	1967	87 ft
EI	175	005	177090073300	Vastar Resources, Inc.	1966	90 ft
EI	175	006	177090073200	Vastar Resources, Inc.	1966	88 ft
EI	175	008	177090089700	Vastar Resources, Inc.	1975	83 ft
EI	175	009	177090090500	Vastar Resources, Inc.	1968	90 ft
EI	175	011	177090086800	Vastar Resources, Inc.	1973	83 ft
EI	175	012	177090087100	Vastar Resources, Inc.	1968	90 ft
EI	175	013	177090088000	Vastar Resources, Inc.	1969	87 ft
EI	179	001	177094088700	Kerr-McGee Corporation	1991	97 ft
EI	215	005	177094016400	PennzEnergy	1976	103 ft
EI	248	001	177094112300	Walter Oil & Gas Corporation	1997	155 ft
EI	294	005	177104126801	TDC Energy Corporation	1991	214 ft
EI	300	003	177104102700	Amoco Production Company	1983	212 ft
EI	301	004	177104134000	Amoco Production Company	1991	232 ft
EI	301	005	177104136700	Amoco Production Company	1994	231 ft
EI	320	003	177104128700	Forest Oil Corporation	1994	244 ft
EI	322	005	177104134100	Amoco Production Company	1996	242 ft
EI	331	004	177104046800	Shell Offshore Inc.	1975	242 ft
EI	331	005	177104047700	Shell Offshore Inc.	1976	242 ft
EI	349	012	177104100500	Marathon Oil Company	1990	337 ft
EI	364	003	177104138000	The Louisiana Land and Exploration Company	1996	357 ft
EW	914	002	608105002200	Tatham Offshore, Inc.	1993	946 ft
EW	917	001	608105006500	Marathon Oil Company	1998	1,195 ft
EW	963	001	608105006000	Marathon Oil Company	1998	1,740 ft
EW	963	002	608105006800	Marathon Oil Company	1998	1,758 ft
EW	965	001	608105006200	British-Borneo Exploration, Inc.	1998	1,694 ft
EW	989	001	608104008600	Kerr-McGee Corporation	1994	565 ft
EW	989	002	608104008701	Kerr-McGee Corporation	1995	565 ft
EW	999	001	608104003202	Placid Oil Company	1989	1,462 ft
EW	1006	002	608105004100	Walter Oil & Gas Corporation	1997	1,884 ft
GB	70	001	608074007000	Newfield Exploration Company	1995	755 ft
GB	70	001	608074007001	Newfield Exploration Company	1997	750 ft

GB	71	002	608074013000	Newfield Exploration Company	1995	750 ft
GB	108	001	608074020600	Kerr-McGee Oil & Gas Corporation	1999	619 ft
GB	117	001	608074013500	Flextrend Development Company	1996	922 ft
GB	117	002	608074014901	Flextrend Development Company	1997	924 ft
GB	134	001	608074062900	ATP	1997	520 ft
GB	152	001	608074020800	Kerr-McGee Oil & Gas Corporation	1999	619 ft
GB	161	001	608074015801	PennzEnergy Exploration and Production, L.L.C.	1999	972 ft
GB	172	B001	608074018200	Shell Offshore Inc.	1998	693 ft
GB	172	B002	608074018401	Shell Offshore Inc.	1999	693 ft
GB	172	B003	608074019700	Shell Offshore Inc.	1999	663 ft
GB	179	001	608074063700	Walter Oil & Gas Corporation	1997	712 ft
GB	216	002	608074081901	Amerada Hess Corporation	1999	1,456 ft
GB	224	005	608074061800	Kerr-McGee Oil & Gas Corporation	1991	742 ft
GB	235	003	608074010600	The Louisiana Land and Exploration Company	1996	785 ft
GB	240	003	608074013100	Mariner Energy, Inc.	1996	832 ft
GB	367	002	608074064100	Mariner Energy, Inc.	1999	1,122 ft
GB	378	002	608074015700	Sonat Exploration GOM Inc.	1997	495 ft
GB	387	SB001	608074014001	EEX Corporation	1996	2,081 ft
GB	388	SA001	608074005400	EEX Corporation	1995	2,097 ft
GB	388	SA002	608074008401	EEX Corporation	1997	2,097 ft
GB	602	A002	608074014401	Shell Deepwater Development Inc.	1999	3,708 ft
GB	602	A005	608074019401	Shell Deepwater Development Inc.	1999	3,693 ft
GC	20	001	608114021300	Reading & Bates Development Co.	1999	880 ft
GC	29	A003	608114009100	Placid Oil Company	1989	1,526 ft
GC	31	004	608114004701	EP Operating Limited Partnership	1988	2,243 ft
GC	31	006	608114009600	EP Operating Limited Partnership	1989	2,234 ft
GC	60	001	608114019800	Mobil Oil Exploration & Producing Southeast Inc.	1996	870 ft
GC	60	002	608114020101	Mobil Oil Exploration & Producing Southeast Inc.	1996	868 ft
GC	72	A001	608115008500	Shell Deepwater Production Inc.	1996	2,040 ft
GC	110	001	608114020600	Shell Offshore Inc.	1996	1,730 ft
GC	113	A002	608115012701	Shell Deepwater Development Inc.	1999	2,045 ft
GC	116	A002	608115008600	Shell Deepwater Production Inc.	1996	2,046 ft
GC	116	A003	608115012200	Shell Deepwater Production Inc.	1998	2,046 ft
GC	136	006	608114020000	Texaco	1995	860 ft
GC	136	007	608114020401	Texaco	1995	1,040 ft
GC	200	TA001	608114021600	BP Exploration & Oil Inc.	1997	2,670 ft
GC	200	TA003	608114021800	BP Exploration & Oil Inc.	1997	2,670 ft
GC	200	TA004	608114021901	BP Exploration & Oil Inc.	1999	2,670 ft
GC	200	TA005	608114020501	BP Exploration & Oil Inc.	1998	2,670 ft
GC	254	004	608115008301	British-Borneo Exploration, Inc.	1999	3,225 ft
GC	254	005	608115009000	British-Borneo Exploration, Inc.	1999	3,234 ft
GI	41	004	177174009600	Vastar Resources, Inc.	1985	100 ft
GI	41	005	177174009500	Vastar Resources, Inc.	1978	91 ft
GI	41	006	177174009700	Vastar Resources, Inc.	1978	91 ft
GI	43	004	177174009800	Vastar Resources, Inc.	1978	114 ft
GI	47	004	177174009300	Vastar Resources, Inc.	1978	88 ft

GI	47	006	177174018500	Vastar Resources, Inc.	1986	97 ft
HI	A 7	004	427044011600	Texaco	1984	120 ft
HI	A 309	007	427114070100	Coastal Oil & Gas Corporation	1995	213 ft
HI	A 320	001	427114077400	Walter	1997	237 ft
HI	A 325	008	427114064000	Pennzoil Exploration and Production Company	1989	231 ft
HI	A 325	009	427114064100	Pennzoil Exploration and Production Company	1989	231 ft
HI	A 370	003	427114065100	Kerr-McGee Oil & Gas Corporation	1993	375 ft
HI	A 373	001	427114065000	EOG Resources, Inc.	1992	375 ft
HI	A 378	001	427114080601	Kerr-McGee	1999	332 ft
HI	A 378	B018	427114075700	Kerr-McGee	1996	360 ft
HI	A 519	004	427094093200	Coastal Oil & Gas Corporation	1991	220 ft
HI	A 573	006	427094053700	Union Oil Company of California	1980	350 ft
HI	A 587	002	427094089602	Panaco, Inc.	1990	467 ft
MC	28	TB002	608174051600	BP Exploration & Oil Inc.	1996	1,853 ft
MC	28	TB005	608174051900	BP Exploration & Oil Inc.	1996	1,853 ft
MC	28	TB006	608174052000	BP Exploration & Oil Inc.	1998	1,853 ft
MC	72	TB001	608174051500	BP Exploration & Oil Inc.	1996	1,853 ft
MC	292	001	608174050900	Texaco	1999	3,405 ft
MC	292	003	608174083201	Texaco	1999	3,393 ft
MC	292	004	608174083301	Texaco	1999	3,393 ft
MC	354	A003	608174044700	Exxon Corporation	1993	1,460 ft
MC	355	A001	608174044900	Exxon Corporation	1993	1,460 ft
MC	355	A002	608174044800	Exxon Corporation	1993	1,458 ft
MC	355	A004	608174084301	Exxon Corporation	1999	1,458 ft
MC	357	002	608174053801	Newfield Exploration Company	1998	445 ft
MC	401	001	608174032901	Kerr-McGee Oil & Gas Corporation	1993	1,367 ft
MC	401	002	608174034600	Kerr-McGee Oil & Gas Corporation	1993	1,700 ft
MC	441	A004	608174037601	EEX Corporation	1993	1,438 ft
MC	441	A009	608174041500	EEX Corporation	1993	1,438 ft
MC	441	B006	608174038400	EEX Corporation	1992	1,531 ft
MC	441	B007	608174040002	EEX Corporation	1993	1,531 ft
MC	441	B008	608174040100	EEX Corporation	1992	1,531 ft
MC	445	001	608174042900	Kerr-McGee Oil & Gas Corporation	1993	2,094 ft
MC	445	002	608174047300	Kerr-McGee Oil & Gas Corporation	1994	2,095 ft
MC	485	A001	608174041600	EEX Corporation	1993	1,438 ft
MC	686	A001	608174054100	Shell Deepwater Production Inc.	1997	5,292 ft
MC	687	A002	608174054000	Shell Deepwater Production Inc.	1998	5,292 ft
MC	730	A003	608174054200	Shell Deepwater Production Inc.	1997	5,295 ft
MC	783	004	608164013401	Shell Deepwater Production Inc.	1993	1,494 ft
MC	807	004	608174038800	Shell Deepwater Production Inc.	1996	2,956 ft
MC	825	005	608164034400	Kerr-McGee Oil & Gas Corporation	1999	1,711 ft
MP	145	005	177254047300	OXY USA Inc.	1989	213 ft
MP	149	002	177254058901	Walter Oil & Gas Corporation	1994	220 ft
MP	260	001	177244081400	Santa Fe Snyder Corporation	1999	315 ft
MP	262	001	177244076100	CXY Energy Offshore Inc.	1996	283 ft
MP	281	001	177244069100	Walter Oil & Gas Corporation	1994	293 ft

MP	291	001	177244056600	Allied Natural Gas Corporation	1995	272 ft
MU	131	001	177254060100	ATP Oil & Gas Corporation	1998	165 ft
MU	A 327	004	427114071200	Hall-Houston Oil Company	1994	220 ft
PN	1010	001	427014005000	Walter	1999	128 ft
SM	61	005	177074029400	Chevron U.S.A. Inc.	1984	130 ft
SM	67	001	177074039000	Cockrell Oil Corporation	1984	130 ft
SS	176	007	177114099800	Chevron U.S.A. Inc.	1990	100 ft
SS	204	001	177110067000	Union Pacific Resources Company	1995	103 ft
SS	204	002	177110067200	Union Pacific Resources Company	1983	100 ft
SS	204	004	177110081400	Union Pacific Resources Company	1969	103 ft
SS	217	002	177110055500	Kerr-McGee Corporation	1971	114 ft
SS	269	005	177124010700	Union Oil Company of California	1976	187 ft
SS	274	001	177122001100	Apache Corporation	1969	219 ft
SS	274	005	177124008600	Apache Corporation	1975	210 ft
SS	276	002	177124058800	Forest Oil Corporation	1998	215 ft
SS	316	002	177124043400	Hall-Houston Oil Company	1991	295 ft
SS	317	001	177124038600	Newfield Exploration Company	1990	295 ft
SS	321	001	177124057000	ATP Oil & Gas Corporation	1997	323 ft
SS	326	001	177124058700	Walter Oil & Gas Corporation	1998	364 ft
SS	361	001	177124054900	Phillips Petroleum Company	1998	405 ft
ST	169	005	177154032600	Samedan Oil Corporation	1980	88 ft
ST	169	006	177154062300	Samedan Oil Corporation	1985	102 ft
ST	177	001	177154007800	Chevron U.S.A. Inc.	1976	144 ft
ST	231	001	177164019900	SOCO Offshore, Inc.	1998	238 ft
VK	28	A008	608164018600	BP Exploration & Oil Inc.	1995	1,290 ft
VK	113	A003	608115013100	Shell Deepwater Development Inc.	1999	1,968 ft
VK	783	005	608164021701	Shell Deepwater Production Inc.	1996	1,142 ft
VK	784	001	608164023200	Shell Deepwater Production Inc.	1996	1,750 ft
VK	825	004	608164033201	Kerr-McGee Oil & Gas Corporation	1998	1,722 ft
VK	862	002	608164021600	Walter Oil & Gas Corporation	1995	1,067 ft
VK	944	001	608164032200	Elf Exploration, Inc.	1997	740 ft
VK	986	001	608164022800	Walter Oil & Gas Corporation	1995	893 ft
VR	215	006	177054028500	Newfield Exploration Company	1979	140 ft
VR	246	009	177054034600	Chevron U.S.A. Inc.	1982	155 ft
VR	302	002	177064021701	CXY Energy Offshore Inc.	1977	197 ft
VR	320	009	177064064200	Oryx Energy Company	1991	206 ft
WC	192	001	177004055500	Diamond Shamrock	1982	54 ft
WC	459	003	177024062900	Conoco Inc.	1985	135 ft
WC	548	001	177024106000	Walter Oil & Gas Corporation	1994	185 ft
WC	584	001	177024085700	Walter Oil & Gas Corporation	1989	237 ft
WC	592	001	177024106301	Walter Oil & Gas Corporation	1995	252 ft
WC	638	001	177024116900	Kerr-McGee Oil & Gas Corporation	1998	373 ft
WD	45	001	177190038200	CXY Energy Offshore Inc.	1959	50 ft
WD	45	002	177190038300	CXY Energy Offshore Inc.	1959	72 ft
WD	45	007	177190038402	CXY Energy Offshore Inc.	1981	50 ft
WD	62	005	177194027900	Mesa Operating	1985	130 ft

WD	70	001	177190062800	Vastar Resources, Inc.	1958	143 ft
WD	70	003	177190063000	Vastar Resources, Inc.	1961	143 ft
WD	71	001	177190061900	Vastar Resources, Inc.	1961	142 ft
WD	77	001	177194065504	ATP Oil & Gas Corporation	1999	187 ft
WD	106	002	177194056800	Walter Oil & Gas Corporation	1995	234 ft
WD	107	001	177194056400	Walter Oil & Gas Corporation	1996	222 ft

www.ingramcontent.com/pod-product-compliance
Lightning Source LLC
Chambersburg PA
CBHW080312290526

45790CB00005B/2013